YOUR
FAI✝H
WILL MAKE YOU
UNSTOPPABLE

I will instruct you and teach in the way you should go;
I will watch over you I will guide you with my eyes.

Psalm 32:8

ISBN 978-0-9969246-9-6

Printed in the United States of America.

TABLE OF CONTENTS

PREFACE

Working on this amazing book project with these powerful women of God has been a pleasure. There is nothing more gratifying than working with like-minded women! It is a wonderful thing! These amazing women have a story that needs to be shared with the world, and this book allows that to happen. Their ability to walk by faith and not by sight is something we can all learn. God has called us to walk by His faith and not by the world's fear. I believe that these stories will be a blessing to all who read them. Matthew 5:16 tells us, "Let your light shine so brightly before men that they will see your good works and glorify your Father which is in heaven."

Hebrew 11:1 says, "Now faith is the substance of things hoped for, the evidence of things not seen." God's love for us, His people, fulfill His message. When we share our stories, it helps people to see what is possible in their lives. Our stories will reveal how our faith in the power of God has made us unstoppable. The word of God always shares with us the importance of walking by faith. By doing this, it gives us the ability to believe in the power to achieve anything our heart desires.

James 1:6 says, "When you ask, you must believe and not doubt because the one who doubts is like a wave of the sea, blown and tossed by the wind."

2 Corinthians 5 says, "We walk by faith and not by sight."

James 1:3 says, "Because you know that the testing of your faith produces perseverance."

I want you to trust your faith in the power of God to get you to your next level of greatness. One thing is for sure, no matter what you are dealing with right now, when you decide to keep your faith in God and trust His promises, all things will work together for your good.

SPECIAL THANKS

I want to thank God for this vision of this powerful book. Thank You for always believing in our power to be great. Thank You, Lord, for showing us how we can be whatever our hearts desire. You have called us to be Awesome, Powerful, Mighty, and Great.

I want to thank every person who has ever believed in our greatness.

I want to thank each of these fantastic women for sharing their stories. Dr. Jacqueline Mohair, Dr. Renee Huffman, Cheryl Morgan Wilson, Rev Dr. Stephanie Castro, Bridget Shaw, Glynnis Thatch, Dr. Pamela Cox, Dr. London Spivey, Dr. Lisa Jones, Dr. Barbara Jackson, Ardra Sinett, Mekita Whitfield, Cynthia Milton, Dr. Harriet Roberson, Dr. Angela Bennett, Dr. Uzo Osili, and Sonji Neverson. Thank You for trusting my vision and saying yes to it. I thank God for every one of you, and I am so honored to know you.

Habakkuk 2:2-3 says: And then God answered me and said, "Write the vision and engrave it so plainly upon tablets that everyone who passes may be able to read it easily and quickly. For the vision is yet for an appointed time it will not deceive or disappoint." Because of the vision God has given me I have written it plainly and you have picked it up and ran with it! To God be the glory.

Thank you, Stephanie Hunt, for using your gift to bring the project to life.

Thank you, Sonia Edwards, for editing this masterpiece.

Dawn Lieck, I want to thank you and your team for helping us successfully launch this amazing book project.

A MESSAGE FROM VISIONARY: DR. NORA SHARIFF-BORDEN

It is such an honor to join these women as we write this masterpiece. The Bible teaches us the importance of being evenly yoked. I am so excited to be yoked with some powerful and amazing women. There is nothing more powerful than connecting with like-minded people; it brings you joy; it puts a smile on your face, it compels you to push yourself to be your best self.

This book is all about walking the walk of Faith which I realize is not always the easy thing to do, but we must learn how to do it. Faith is the one thing that will allow us to reach the full potential that God has for us. We must learn always to execute our Faith. That's why it is important for us to learn how to walk by Faith and not sight.

Faith shows us how to get where we are going. It is sad when people do not know where they are going. Yogi Berra said that "If you don't know where you are going, you'll end up someplace else." I want you to think about how you are going to execute your Faith. I want you to know that God has designed us for greatness. 1Peter 2:9 tells us, "But you are a chosen race, a royal priesthood, a holy nation, a people for His own possession, that you may proclaim the excellencies of Him who called you out of darkness into His marvelous light!"

Genesis 12:2 "And I will make of you a great nation, and I will bless you and make your name great so that you will be a blessing!

These scriptures tell us that God has designed us with greatness in mind; all we need to do is walk by Faith and not by sight. We must be careful not to allow what others do not see in us and stay focused on what God sees in us.

I love what my friend Crisette Ellis says "You must dare to see what we do not see. If you do not see greatness, then greatness will not appear!" I know we have been chosen for greatness; we decide to step into it daily!

I read something not too long ago that said, "When Fear comes knocking on your door, Faith answers and says no one is home."

I want you to enjoy this great masterpiece of collaboration with some powerful writers.

I want you to focus on these scriptures every day.

Scriptures:
Romans 10:17 Faith comes from hearing and hearing by the word of God.

Hebrews 11:6 It is impossible to please God without Faith. Anyone who wants to come to Him must believe that God exists and that He rewards those who seek Him.

Ephesians 2:8-9 For it is by grace you have been saved through Faith, and this is not from yourself, it is the gift of God not by works so that no one can boast.

DR. NORA SHARIFF-BORDEN

Dr. Nora Shariff-Borden was born and raised in Boston, Massachusetts, along with her three younger sisters. Nora and her husband, Neil, presently live outside of Atlanta, Georgia. Together they have six adult children, 14 grandchildren, and three great-grandchildren.

For 18 years, Nora was a practicing Muslim, trying to find out who God was. Little did she know that God's plan for her life did not include the Islamic faith. The seed of Christianity was planted in her over thirty-two years ago.

Nora has accepted her call from God to become a Christian inspirational speaker.

"I am the founder and CEO of BWOTMFG, which is an organization that inspires and encourages women to be business owners and helps current businesswomen who may be stuck to become clear about their goals and dreams and how to achieve them! I also host a weekly online show, Real Conversations With Nora, which focuses on the many issues that women face every day through transparent conversations. I dig deep to help women talk about their issues to help them reclaim their authentic selves, and overcome their obstacles so they can navigate through life successfully. Most importantly we have a good time!"

Nora believes she has a gift from God that allows her to connect with women. She believes that if you can touch the heart of a woman, she will do all she can to support you. Nora's goal is to teach women that their words have the power to change their lives. She also believes she can help them paint a picture of what they want their life to look like so that when it appears, all they must do is step into it.

Nora started Business Women On The Move For God because she loves to see women own their greatness and learn how to walk in it every day! She wants the next generation of young businesswomen to realize their greatness and be unapologetic about it! Nora wants women to be able to get up when they have fallen and to learn the importance of continuing their journey!

Nora is a woman with a serious mission who believes that if she meets a women's true needs with total sincerity and commitment to serve, as God has called her to do, her work will not be in vain.

Her outcome and projection for the future of BWOTMFG are to establish a $10,000 scholarship program for young women who major in business!

"Great things happen when people have Great Expectations!"

Instagram @bwotmfg, Facebook @BusinessWomenontheMoveforGod, and on YouTube or Spotify at Nora Shariff! You can also visit my website at https://www.bwotmfg.com/.

Dr. Nora Shariff-Borden
Founder and CEO of BWOTMFG
Stone Mountain, GA
470-553-4107
info@bwotmfg.com

WHAT IS FAITH ALL ABOUT

by Dr. Nora Shariff-Borden

One of the things I have personally come to realize is that my Faith is like a muscle that I must always execute. There have been many times in my life when I did not execute my Faith. I was too busy focusing on the situation that I was faced with that I could not recognize the presence of the Lord. I realized I needed to grow in my Faith to see God working on my behalf.

One thing I always tell others is that God has a sense of humor, especially when He is getting ready to test our Faith. I believe it is a test to see if we trust Him enough to come through for us. What I have learned is that it is better to trust in His power. My Faith has been strengthened over the years, and I have learned to trust in Him and not lean on my understanding. I had to learn God knows my beginning and my end. Faith is all about trusting God. No matter what I don't see, none of that matters when I have God on my side. He wants us to have Faith in Him and not anything else. I have learned if I am going to fully trust Him, then I can't worry about the situation.

According to His word, He has told me to be anxious for nothing, but in everything by prayer and supplication, with thanksgiving, let your request be made known to God; and the peace of God which surpasses all understanding will guard your hearts and minds through Christ Jesus. Philippians 4:6-7

Here God is telling us that we do not need to worry because He has everything under control. Well, why, then, do we worry? The answer to that is we want to be in control. I have learned that I can't control anything, and the more I refuse to give everything over to Him, I will always stay in a state of confusion. The word of God says He works all things together for good for those who love Him and are called to His purpose. Romans 8:2

Let me share a couple of my faith stories with you. My first walk of Faith was when my youngest daughter was pregnant with her second child, who was trying to come early. They admitted her to the hospital. I can remember the Holy Spirit told me to take my oil and go to the hospital, and He would tell me what to say once I got there. His instructions were clear. I began to lay hands on her and pray that she would stay inside the womb until the appointed time, and she was born on the exact due date, which was June 15th. On that day, Nia Simone made her presence to the world.

The second walk of the Faith was when they diagnosed my husband with Colon Cancer, and you notice that I said they because, until this day, I have never confessed that he had cancer. When the doctor told us her diagnosis, I looked at her and said I know that God gives you wisdom and knowledge, but you are never going to hear me say that my husband has cancer. Because my God is a healer, and He is going to heal my husband. I called my prayer warrior friends and told them to pray. I instructed them on what I wanted them to pray; I told them not to add anything or take anything away, just pray the prayer I had given them to pray. And they did! That was 16 years ago. The prayers of the righteous availeth much. That means God pays attention when the righteous start to pray. When you make up your mind to walk by Faith, you become unstoppable. What I need is for you to walk by Faith and decide to be unstoppable.

The three young Jewish men (Shadrach, Meshach, and Abed-Nego) who refused to bow to the image, told King Nebuchadnezzar: "If that is the case, our God whom we serve can deliver us from the burning fiery furnace, and He will deliver us from your hand, O king. But if not, let it be known to you, O king, that we do not serve your gods, nor will we worship the gold image which you have set up" (Daniel 3:17-18). They had Faith in their God that He would deliver them, and He did. They chose not to look at what they saw; that is what true Faith is.

The woman with the issue of blood; had issues with bleeding for twelve years and had suffered from many things. She had spent all her money on physicians, and nothing got better; in fact, it got worse. I believe that she heard that Jesus was coming to town. She had Faith and believed if she could just touch the hem of His garment, she could be healed. She stepped behind Jesus and touched the hem of His garment, and instantly she was healed. That is what true Faith does.

Isaiah 54: 17 tells us that no weapon formed against us shall prosper. It is our Faith that will give us confidence that it shall not prosper. He did not promise that it wouldn't come, but He did promise that it would not prosper.

1 Peter 1: 8-9 "Though you have not seen him, you love him; and even though you do not see him now, you believe in him and are filled with an inexpressible and glorious joy, for you are receiving the result of your

faith, the salvation of your souls."

This scripture helps us to see even though we can't physically see Him; we have Faith that He exists.

James 2:14 Faith without works is dead. What does it profit us if we say we have Faith but do not have works?" This tells us that if we work but do not have Faith, our work is dead. This means we must continue to work even if we don't see the evidence; we must not stop working. That is the example of Faith without works is dead.

Our Faith is increased when we draw closer to the Lord. We don't need Faith when everything is going well; it is in the tough times that we need to call on our Faith. It is so easy for us to talk about how faithful we are until we are faced with life issues. That is when we see what we are made of during those tough times. Faith says Lord, I trust you.

Proverbs 3:5-6 says Trust in the Lord with all your heart and lean not on your own understanding. The key here is to trust in the Lord, not what we think. When we connect with the things of God, when we see things from God's perspective, this is when we will have a full understanding of what Faith is all about and what it means to trust in the Lord.

Now I must be honest with you. There have been times when I found it hard to trust the process God was taking me through. It wasn't until I had gone through the process that I realized what He was doing. I had to learn to trust the process that God was taking me through. I had to realize that He knew what was best for me, better than I knew myself.

That's why it is important for us to build a solid relationship with the Lord. When we do that, it is so much easier to trust the process, and He takes us through it. So often, we want to seek others for advice instead of seeking God first, for He is the one who can guide us and instruct us. Psalms 32:8 tells us, "The Lord will instruct us and teach in the way we should go." He promises to counsel us and watch over us and show us the way we should go.

Scripture: Galatians 3:26-27 So in Christ Jesus you are all children of God through Faith, for all of you who were baptized into Christ have clothed yourselves with Christ.

How did you feel when your Faith was being tested?

Were there times when you found it tough to trust the process God was taking you through?

Are You trusting more what others have to say about you than you are God?

WHEN YOU HAVE FAITH IN GOD, YOU REALIZE ALL THINGS ARE POSSIBLE

by Dr. Nora Shariff-Borden

Hebrew 11:1 -
Now faith is being sure of what we hope for and certain of what we don't see.
The Amplified version puts it this way; Now faith is the assurance (the confirmation, the title deed) of the things (we) hope for, being the proof of things (we) do not see, and the conviction of their reality. (Faith perceiving as real fact what is not revealed to the senses).

Hebrew 11:6 -
And without faith, it is impossible to please God because anyone who comes to Him must believe that He exists and that He rewards those who earnestly seek Him. The Amplified version puts it this way; But without faith, it is impossible to please and be satisfactory to Him, for whoever would come near to God must (necessarily) believe that God exists and that He is a rewarder of those who earnestly and diligently seek Him out!

You must know that faith travels where the eyes can't travel. Faith pleases God. Having faith says, Lord, I trust in you even when I can't see where you are taking me. It allows me to lean on you when what I see is cloudy. It is being sure of what I am hoping for and certain of what I do not see.

When I trust in the Lord, I don't lean on my understanding, but I trust that God will turn things around for my good. It helps me to see that all things work together for my good. God loves when we operate in faith. I believe it makes Him smile. God's desire is that we look to Him for everything. He wants to supply all our needs. My thought is the greater our faith, the greater our blessing.

It requires some action from us. We must put our faith into motion. It is a requirement on our behalf that says we must constantly be working on our faith. I believe this shows God that we trust Him. It helps us to realize that all things are possible for us with God.

It is easy to have faith when everything is going our way. It is in the tough times that we see what we are made of. This is when we see our faith at work. It is important that we understand that it is in the valley where we learn our lesson. This is where we walk by faith and not by sight. It is where our lives are transformed.

Our faith teaches us to remain positive about our life, and it reassures us of God's great outcome for us. When we have passed the great test of faith, God allows us to tell our story on the mountaintop (that is your testimony). I always tell people that the valley is where we learn our lessons in life, and the mountain is where we tell our story. The Bible is the best book in the world, it is our manual for life, and it is where God speaks to us. It can help us with every situation we will ever face in life. All we must do is listen to God's word and ask the Lord to help us to see that our faith requires work. We must study the word and master its power. What I have realized, when I study the word, my faith is increased, which allows me to put it to work. Faith without works is dead. Our desire should be to have a line of faith that is always working.

Scripture:
Mark 11:24 Therefore, I tell you, whatever you ask for in prayer, believe that you have received it, and it will be yours.

Can God Trust Your Faith?

Does Your Faith Match Your Work?

Do You Have a Vision for Your Life?

Is Your Faith Allowing You to Remain Positive About Your Vision?

HERE ARE 12 WAYS YOUR FAITH WILL MAKE YOU UNSTOPPABLE!

by Dr. Nora Shariff-Borden

1. Faith is stored in your heart and spoken through your mouth. Proverbs 23:7 "As a man thinketh in his heart, so is he."

2. Always keep the two working together. Believe with your heart, and say what you believe with your mouth. Isaiah 55:11 "So is my word that goes out from my mouth, it will not return to me empty, but will accomplish what I desire and achieve the purpose for which I sent it."

3. What consistently goes into the heart will eventually come out of the mouth. Proverbs 18:21 "The tongue has the power of life and death."

4. Always believe in the promises of God and not your circumstances. Jeremiah 29:11 "For I know the plans I have for you," declares the Lord, "Plans to prosper you and not to harm you, plans to give you hope and a future."

5. Keep speaking the truth with your mouth; it doesn't matter what you see. Hebrews 11:6 "and without Faith, it is impossible to please God, because anyone who comes to Him must believe that He exists and that He rewards those who earnestly seek Him."

6. Faith is the substance of the things hoped for but certain of what we do not see. What that says is you don't have to see it; you must believe it will happen. Hebrews 11:1 "Now Faith is being sure of what we hope for and certain of what we do not see."

7. Boldly confess what you believe. Acts 4:29 "Your servants speak your words with great boldness."

8. We must learn to call those things as God would call them in our lives! Romans 4:17 "And call things that are not as though they were."

9. Faith is expressed by our words, so we must watch the words that come out of our mouths. John 15:7 "If you remain in me and my words remain in you, ask whatever you wish, and it will be given you."

10. Don't waver when things are not going well; hold fast to your confession of Faith. It will cause you to rise above your circumstances.

Palms 62:1-2 "My soul finds rest in God alone; My salvation comes from Him. He alone is my rock and my salvation: He is my fortress, and I will never be shaken."

11. Allow Faith to rule in your life and not circumstances or logic.
Proverbs 3:5-6 "trust in the Lord with all your heart and lean not on your own understanding; in all your ways acknowledge Him, and He will make your paths straight."

12. Hang around those that have the same kind of Faith that you do. (This is your circle of influence.)
Acts 4:32 "All believers were one in heart and mind."

I love what Pastor Andre' Gorham says in his book, "Faith Works The Dynamics of Believing."
Have you experienced the power of believing?
Have you built a strong foundation for your Faith?
Make certain you are totally convinced that God's word is not only true but that it is speaking directly to you! Declare the name of Jesus, and believe what you are saying will come into reality. When these are linked with an active prayer life, God graciously unlocks His storehouse of abundance and blessings upon you!

Start thanking God through the word, and it will build your confidence in your Faith.

- Lord, thank you that no weapon formed against me shall prosper.
- Lord, I am thankful that I am fearfully and wonderfully made by you.
- Lord, thank you that I have not thrown away my confidence, for it will richly reward me.
- Lord, I will rejoice, for you have done marvelous things.
- Lord, I can do all things through you who has strengthened me.
- Lord, thank you that there is nothing impossible for you.
- This is the day that the Lord has made, and I will rejoice and be glad in it.
- We must learn to master the power God has given us through His word!
- I want you to make a commitment to God that you will begin to see yourself the way He sees you, which is powerful and great.
- Make a list of 50 reasons why you deserve all that God has for you.

Scripture: I pray that out of His glorious riches, He may strengthen you with power through His Spirit in your inner being, so that Christ may dwell in your hearts through Faith; that you, being rooted and established in love. Ephesians 3:16-17

Is your Faith stored up in your heart and spoken through your mouth? (Be honest with yourself)

Are you focused on your circumstances or God? Who is the only one that can fix them?

Are you speaking the truth with your mouth daily?

Are you allowing Faith to rule in your life daily?

WAYS TO CHANGE YOUR THOUGHTS AND BUILD YOUR FAITH

by Dr. Nora Shariff-Borden

You can choose to be poor or prosperous; it is a state of mind.

The change starts in your mind. It is simple to change the way you think. It is a personal choice.

Now is the time to choose to change your life, do it now, don't wait.

Fear and uncertainty deserve no place in your mind.

Change is necessary.

To get someplace you've never been or to be someone you've never been, you must do something you've never done.

What you allow between your left and right ear will determine your thoughts.

None of this will work for you if you don't control your thoughts.

Decide to change, and don't get caught in negative thoughts.

If you get caught up in a step-by-step plan, you're going to find yourself worrying about potential roadblocks that you will encounter, and when you allow that to happen, it leads to fear and uncertainties. The key is to walk by faith and not by what you see because what you see doesn't count when it comes to faith.

For every problem you encounter, if you walk by faith, God will show you at least ten solutions.

You have the power to change your thoughts. It all resides inside you. All you must do is believe and have faith in all your gifts and abilities.

Your thoughts become habitual thinking, and that can be good or bad; the choice is yours. God has gifted you with the power.

Life is a self-fulfilling prophecy. We get what we expect! So, ask yourself what are you expecting God to do in your life?

Whether you think you can or whether you think you can't, you are right either way!

90% of the outside data that feeds into your conscious mind daily is negative, and fear feeds on that. Think about what would happen if you made that 90% positive where your life would be.

We move in the direction of our dominant thoughts. That is why it is important to focus on the positive things that will cause your mind to move in the direction of your greatness.

Don't get caught up in the "How To." Learn to leave the "how to" up to God, for He is the one who makes all things possible. Whenever you find yourself trying to figure it all out, I want you to stop and remember who is in charge.

Decide first to have faith in God's ability to solve your problems. You will be surprised how fast that can and will happen.

Once you decide to change, God will open all kinds of doors for you if you don't give up. The key is to have faith and never give up.

Scripture: 2 Corinthians 5:7 For we live by faith, not by sight.

How are you changing your thoughts?

What data are you feeding yourself? Is it positive or negative?

What are you willing to change that has not been beneficial to you?

Are you willing to acknowledge the power you have inside you?

FAITH WILL ALLOW YOU TO LET GO AND LET GOD!

by Dr. Nora Shariff-Borden

My mind is a powerfully formative tool that helps me shape my own experiences. As I open my mind to the wisdom and faith of Jesus, I change my thoughts, reasoning, perception, and feelings, and I recollect my spiritual power. Faith allows the results to become life-transforming. Our minds must be transformed to let go of stuff that bogs us down.

Romans 12:2
Do not be conformed to this world but be transformed by the renewal of your mind. Then you will be able to test and approve what God's will is, His good and pleasing and perfect will.

When we walk in faith and we let go, we release all concern and cease struggling. As we open our minds and our lives to the divine wisdom and power of God, it will prepare us to walk by faith and receive the abundant blessings of Jesus Christ.

Letting go and letting God allows us to have faith in the power of God which allows us to turn our challenges into opportunities and concerns into hope. As we realize Jesus is the source of all our wisdom and blessings, connecting totally with the presence of Jesus, we can fulfill our spirit, mind, and body.

Letting go and letting God may not always be the easiest thing to do, but it is for sure the best thing we can do.

I love the fact that God is letting us know that He will fully satisfy every need of ours according to His riches in glory in Christ Jesus. This gives us the confidence that God is with us. He is helping us, and He is guiding us all through life.

Scripture:
Philippians 4:19 And my God will fully satisfy every need of yours according to his riches in glory in Christ Jesus.

Letting go is not always the easy thing to do, but it is a must. Do you agree?

How willing are you to let go and let God?

Do you believe that your mind is powerful and that you can change it?

Are you ready to transform your mind?

TAKE CONTROL OF YOUR POWER BY FAITH

by Dr. Nora Shariff-Borden

We can't overcome our weaknesses and fears because the enemy will always focus on our weaker points. Since our minds are the battlefield for the enemies' tactics, those tactics will always be directed toward our thinking. Instead of focusing on our faith which brings us the strength of the Lord, we focus on our weakness which causes us to speak words of doubt, fear, and lack, comparing ourselves with others. These are all the arrows that the enemy uses to control our lives and our thoughts.

Isaiah 55:11 tells us, "That my words that go out of my mouth will not return to me empty, but they will accomplish what I send them out to do." And then Proverbs 18:21 lets us know that "There is life and death in the power of the tongue.

My question to you is, are you speaking death into your life by telling yourself untruths? Nobody likes me, I am shy, that may work for you, you're great with people, I don't like people, or I am too fat, I am lazy, I am too scared. The list could go on and on. God tells us to speak the truth in our lives, which comes from having faith in His word. For example, Phil 4:13 "We can do all things through Christ who strengthens us," and Phil 4:19 NIV "My God will meet all my needs according to His glorious riches in Christ Jesus." Matt 7:7, Ask, and it will be given to you. What is God saying? Whatever you need, ask me in faith, and you shall have it.

But there is a requirement: we must believe that by faith, He can do it. Finally in Deut. 8:18 God reminds us that He has given us the ability to produce wealth. I believe we can only produce wealth when we work for ourselves; working for others will never produce wealth for you. When that person decides they no longer need you, then your wealth is gone. One thing is for sure; you will never let yourself go. The bottom line is, God is our source of faith.

Scripture: James 1:6 But when you ask, you must believe and not doubt, because the one who doubts is like a wave of the sea, blown and tossed by the wind.

What do you need to take control of in your life?

Do you believe in your ability to be great?

What are the things that are holding you back?

What are some of the things you need to let go of in your life that you know are holding you back?

THE BEST IS YET TO COME WHEN YOU WALK BY FAITH

by Dr. Nora Shariff-Borden

What are you waiting for? Your best will never show up if you don't expect it to!

In the book of Deuteronomy 3:24, God says Oh Lord God, you have only begun to show your servant your Greatness and your strong hand: for what God is there in the heavens and in the earth that can do according to your works and according to your might?

Our Greatness will only show up when we are ready for it.

In Ephesians 1:19, God says What is the exceeding Greatness of His power towards those who believe?

Remember, if you are breathing, it is never too late to follow God's best for you! The key is you must walk by faith and not what you see. It takes faith to follow your best and courage to reach It!

Whatever the mind of a woman can conceive and believe and have faith in, she can achieve whatever her heart desires.

I have realized that faith belongs to those who believe in her! When you have strong faith, she will always show you when you need her.

I want you to know that you are destined by your faith to have all that you desire to have in life. Don't allow others to bully you out of your Greatness. Your Greatness is earned and never given to you for free! If you want it, you must work for it!"

No one can ever steal your Greatness unless you give it to them! So, never share your dreams with those who are not on the same page as you are!

Are you willing to stand up for what you want out of life?

It is so important that you expect the best to happen in your life!

What excuses are you selling your Greatness? "Excuses are the lies we are telling ourselves to keep us from dealing with the truth!"

Ask yourself this question! What would Greatness say to you when you meet her?

Know that someone will always have a problem with your Greatness! That means you must make sure the people in your circle are ok with your Greatness! For it is your Greatness that will reveal to you the best that is headed your way.

It is important to make sure you are always moving forward toward your Greatness! Deciding to walk into your Greatness with great faith no matter what life throws your way is the key thing that will allow your dreams to become your reality.

In the book of Psalms 32:8, God says, "I will instruct you and teach you the way to go. I will watch over you and guide you with my eyes!"

The key point to reaching our best, we must be willing to follow the instruction of the Lord by Faith.
If we don't, we are headed down a dead-end street that leads us to nowhere.

I love what Bishop T.D. Jakes says, "When you hold on to your history, you do it at the expense of your destiny and your greatness."

Know that faith is the key that unlocks the door to our dreams, courage, and Greatness.

Scripture: James 1:3 Because you know that the testing of your faith produces perseverance.

Are you willing to release what others think about you?

Are you willing to follow the instruction of the Lord?

How hard is it for you to walk in your faith?

Who do you call first when you are faced with a life challenge, your friends or God?

FAITH DOESN'T MAKE THINGS EASY, BUT IT DOES MAKE THEM POSSIBLE

by Dr. Nora Shariff-Borden

I recently read something that said that faith doesn't make things easy. It makes them possible. Luke 1:37

Wow, this is a mouth full and powerful all at the same time. The Bible teaches us in John 16:33, "I have told you these things. So that you may have peace in this world, you will have trouble. But take heart! I have overcome the world.

"Faith says that with God, all things are possible!"

1 Peter 5:10, "And the God of all Grace, who called you to His eternal glory in Christ, after you have suffered a little while, will himself restore you and make you strong."

I read something from the Grand Canyon University Website. "There are so many difficulties in life, and we are constantly going through trials and tribulations, no matter if they are big or small. Sometimes we feel like we will never get through a certain situation or never complete a task because they seem impossible. However, nothing is impossible with God by your side."

Life was never meant to be easy. The older we get; the harder life gets. Nobody has life figured out completely, and nobody gets through life easily. We all have struggles. We may not have the same struggles, but we all have our own things to get through. We deal with sickness, loss of loved ones, financial problems, and so many other things, and it is never easy. We all must go through school and graduate and find jobs and try to figure out what we want to do with our lives and who we want to spend it with. We are always worrying about the future and trying to predict what the future holds, but that is impossible and something that only God knows.

But with faith in Christ Jesus, we can overcome all life challenges that we may face in our lives. His desire is to see us through all of life's ups and downs.

Reading all these powerful words makes me think that in life, we all face trouble and sickness, but I know that the God we serve can heal us no matter what our situations are. Think about all the trials and tribulations you have been through in life, some of which you probably don't even remember. That's because trouble doesn't always last; the only way it will last is when we make it our focus. The word of God tells us, "Count it all joy, my brothers, when you meet trials of various kinds, for you know that the testing of your faith produces steadfastness. And let steadfastness have its full effect, that you may be perfect and complete, lacking in nothing." – James 1:2-4.

When my nephew Keone drowned trying to save the life of another kid, and they both lost their lives, I can remember the Lord speaking to me, saying he sacrificed his life just like I gave mine to save the world. I must tell you that it brought me such peace, the kind of peace that the Lord promised would surpass all understanding. I will never forget that beautiful feeling I felt when the Lord spoke those words to me.

Then when my other nephew committed suicide, that was one of the hardest things my family had to go through. I have to say, if it had not been for the Lord on my side, I don't know that I would have gotten through it all. My faith made it possible to get through that storm.

On October 30th, 2021, I lost my mom. For some reason, I had in my mind she was going to live forever. I guess because she was healthy, she walked 4-5 miles every day. When she turned 88, she slowed down a little, but she continued to walk every day. Her cause of death was ruled as a natural cause. I have had the hardest time dealing with her not being here. There is not a day that goes by that I don't think of her and miss her. I can't explain it. I feel like I am in a bad dream, and I would wake up, and she would be here. But it has been my faith that has made it all possible for me to get through.

"And we know that for those who love God all things work together for good, for those who are called according to his purpose."
– Romans 8:28

Even though all the things I have gone through or things you have gone through or might be going through, the best thing we can do is trust God.

Because all things work together in the end, even when we can't see it, because that is what real faith is all about. When everything is good, we forget to thank God. But when things are bad, we want to go running to Him for help. The point is we should always thank Him, good or bad.

I read this from the Grand Canyon University Website. "People will try to deceive you and make it seem like they have life all figured out, but they do not. Nobody is perfect, and nobody is living their life exactly the way they are trying to portray. Social media is what everyone documents their life on, but they only show the good parts, which makes people believe their lives are perfect. Nobody shows their imperfections or messy times in their lives. They use filters to cover up their flaws to make their lives seem better on social media than they are."

Not that I have already obtained this or am already perfect, but I press on to make it my own because Christ Jesus has made me his own. Brothers, I do not consider that I have made it my own. But one thing I do: forgetting what lies behind and straining forward to what lies ahead, I press on toward the goal for the prize of the upward call of God in Christ Jesus. Let those of us who are mature think this way, and if in anything you think otherwise, God will reveal that also to you.   Philippians 3:12-15

This tells me that none of us are perfect. But what we need to be is honest about where we are and deal with it and move on so that we can be where God wants us to be.

We don't need to be discouraged when tough times come. All things are possible with God; He will get us through any hard times. We just need to let Him do so. Know that life's journey may not be easy, but if we trust in the power of the Lord, He will see us through everything.

Although faith makes things possible, it is the power of prayer that allows us to get through to God! So, with faith and prayer on your side, there is no way you will not come out on the other side shining like gold! Prayer is the covenant of all things. Once you open that door, you will see that all things are possible.

Do you believe that everything works together when you are going through it?

Do you use your faith to get you through?

Do you find it hard to overcome your life challenges?

What do you think your ability, or your inability says about your faith?

HOW DO YOU WALK BY FAITH?

by Dr. Nora Shariff-Borden

I believe in walking by faith; you must trust the power of God. You might be asking; how do you do that? You do that through prayer. I want to share a powerful method with you that I read in a little booklet called The Power of Positive Thinking by Norman Vincent Peale. The title of this method is called Prayerize, Pictureize, and Actualize. He goes on to share to ensure something worthwhile happens, first pray about it, and test it according to God's will. Then print a picture of it in your mind as happening, holding the picture firmly in your consciousness. Continue to surrender the picture to God's will, put the matter in God's hands and follow God's guidance.

Work hard and intelligently, thus doing your part to achieve success. Practice believing and continue to hold the picture in your thoughts. Do this, and you will be astonished at the amazing ways in which the picture comes to pass. "That which you have "prayerized" and "Picturized" "Actualizes" our reality. When we do that, we condition ourselves to invoke the power of God upon it, which again helps us see the manifestation of God's power. I want to share an amazing story that I read from a powerful little book. A woman discovered that her husband was drifting away from her. Theirs had been a happy marriage, but the wife had become preoccupied with social affairs, and the husband had gotten busy with his work. Before they knew it, the close, old-time companionship was lost. One day she discovered his interest in another. She became hysterical. She consulted her minister, who instructed her how to pray and to "picturize." He also advised her to hold a mental image of the restoration of the old-time companionship, to visualize the goodness in her husband, and to picture a restored harmony between the two of them. She was instructed to hold that picture with faith.

By this time, her husband had informed her that he wanted a divorce. She had conquered hysteria and calmly replied that she was willing if he wanted it but suggested a deferral of the decision: "If at the end of ninety days you still want a divorce, I will cooperate." He gave her a quizzical look, for he had expected an outburst. Night after night, he went out, and night after night, she sat at home, but she pictured him in his old chair. She even pictured him drying the dishes as he did when they were first married. She visualized the two of them playing golf together as they once had. She maintained this picture with steady faith, and one night there he was, sitting in his chair. Occasionally he would be gone, but on more and more nights, he sat in his chair. Then one Saturday afternoon, he asked," What do you say to a game of golf?" The day went by pleasantly until she realized that the ninetieth day had arrived, so that evening, she said quietly, "Bill, this is the ninetieth day." "What do you mean," he asked, puzzled, "the ninetieth day?" She replied, "Why don't you remember? We agreed to wait ninety days to settle that divorce matter, and this is the day." He looked at her for a moment, then, hidden behind his paper, turned a page, saying, "Don't be silly. I couldn't possibly get along without you. Where did you ever get the idea, I was going to leave you?" By applying this technique, she saved her marriage. This is what it means to walk by faith. Just imagine if we use this technique in every area of our lives. We need to pray to God our Father and Friend. Prayerize it, Picturized it, Actualize it is happening. Then watch God work on our behalf. This story shows what it means to walk by faith.

When we execute our faith daily, we will see and experience the power of God in our lives. So, as you read this amazing story on prayer and faith, think about what you need to do. Prayerize it, Picturized it, Actualize it and then turn it over to God.

Scripture: Romans 8:31 If God is for us, who can be against us?

Does this story show you the importance of what it means to walk by faith and not by sight?

How are you executing your faith daily?

Do you realize that God is with you, God is helping you, and God is guiding you?

Where do you need to practice having greater faith?

WOMEN OF GREAT FAITH

by Dr. Nora Shariff-Borden

Lydia was one of the most successful businesswomen in the Bible. You will find her story in the Bible in Acts 16:14-15. According to Biblical records, Lydia was a businesswoman who dyed and sold purple cloth, a material used by the wealthy and elite of the day. This meant Lydia worked in a high-priced market with a high-end target market.

But Lydia was more than just a woman who sold luxury goods to the elite and the powerful. From all accounts, it appears she was also the head of her household, an employer of others, and a woman of the great Christian faith. She was the first European convert to Christianity and the first to establish a church in her home for other Christians. Fellowship times included exam-ples of how to do business and worship as a part of a businesswoman's day.

As a powerful woman of God, Lydia has much to offer today's Christian businesswomen. Here are seven valuable lessons for women of God from the bible woman, Lydia.

1. Keep prayer in your daily activities. The bible story of Lydia says she met the Apostle Paul at a place of prayer. She also opened her home to have worship services for others. Keep your priorities in order as a woman of God. Remember to pray unceasingly about everything, including your busi-ness activities, by making prayer a priority activity on your daily schedule.

2. Work to please the Lord. Lydia took her responsibility as a Christian businesswoman to work "as unto the Lord" very seriously. You can show Christian beliefs through your nature and personality without being pushy or unprofessional. Show biblical principles through your actions and deci-sions in your business.

3. Design a powerful company. Lydia was a no-nonsense businesswoman who built a major company in a wealthy market. Nothing says a woman of God must play small in the business world. Christian businesswomen should be open to working in all types of industries and not shy away from the potential of going big. If you are pursuing big dreams, use Lydia as your role model for growth.

4. Try non-traditional opportunities. By being a successful and wealthy

merchant of purple cloth, Lydia was in a non-traditional business category during her time. Don't shy away from embracing non-traditional business opportunities. Consider working in fields where few, if any, women are al-ready excelling and create new paths to success.

5. Find your balance between work and home. Lydia maintained her household even while running a powerful business. Each woman must find a way to balance keeping her home in order while running a business. It might mean downsizing or hiring help. Use your business skills to figure out what works for you to get it all done.

6. Learn to grow your business. Lydia's business was so successful that she had to hire employees. Growing a business means eventually needing to hire help. That help might come in the form of a part-time assistant, inde-pendent contractors, freelancers, or full-time employees. Start in the initial business planning stages to consider how and when you will start to hire help so you can expand your business operations. This creates jobs for oth-ers, increases the economy of your area, and increases your status and influ-ence as a business professional.

7. Know you can be prosperous. Lydia shows that successful Christian women can be highly prosperous. There's no reason to fear money or to shy away from earning large amounts of money in business. The important key is to keep a check on your heart, so money does not become your focus in-stead of God. Lydia was a businesswoman in the Bible who prospered while giving all glory to God.
- Article by Charles Wundengba

I believe sister Lydia was a woman of great faith. And because of her faith, God blessed her and gave her favor in many areas of her life.

Queen Vashti, in my eyes, was a powerful woman who loved God. The scripture 1 Corinthians 6:19-20, "Your body is a temple of the Holy Spirit within you, whom you have from God," speaks volumes about how Queen Vashti felt. I believe she was not willing to expose herself to the King and his drunken friend. She valued who she was as a woman, and I believe she was considering what the other women that she represented would feel and think about her if she surrendered to the King's request.

Vashti's refusal to obey the summons of her drunken husband has been ad-mired as heroic in many feminist interpretations of the Book of Esther. Ear-ly feminists admired Vashti's principles and courage. Harriet Beecher Stowe called Vashti's disobedience the "first stand for women's rights." Elizabeth Cody Stanton wrote that Vashti "added new glory to [her] day and generation...by her disobedience; for 'Resistance to tyrants is obedience to God.'

Some more recent feminist interpreters of the Book of Esther compare Vashti's character and actions favorably to those of her successor, Esther, who is traditionally viewed as the heroine of the Purim story.

Saving the Jewish people was important, but I believe that Vashti realized she was a part of a greater plan, and that was to play a part in God's master plan. Let's be clear, there was a greater plan, and if Queen Vashti had sur-rendered to the King, there would be no Queen Esther story. So, my thought is Queen Vashti played a big role in saving the Jewish people. She realized she needed to stand up for the right of women. She was willing to sacrifice her position to do what was right in the sight of God and His peo-ple. The King's friends didn't like Queen Vashti because they knew she was a strong woman, and they were intimidated by the power that they saw in her; they saw her as a threat.

I think what has impressed me the most about Queen Vashti is her wisdom, her confidence, and her ability to take charge of her own life, not surrender-ing to the ideas of others. I believe she laid the foundation for Queen Es-ther. I believe that hearing about the Queen gave Esther the courage to do what she was called to do by contributing to saving the Jewish people. The success of one woman always opens the door for the success of all women; it somehow gives us the courage to fight for the rights of all women. Queen Vashti showed the women that they did not have to settle for seconds and that they could have the best of what God had for them. This is also for us in this season.

Mary The mother of Jesus was a righteous woman; she accepted and sur-rendered to the request of the Holy Spirit. An angel told her she would be-come the mother of the Savior through the Holy Spirit. Despite the poten-tial shame, she submitted and gave birth to Jesus. She and Joseph married, serving as parents to the Son of God.

During her life, Mary bore much sorrow, including watching her son cruci-fied on Calvary. But she also saw him raised from the dead. Mary is revered as a loving influence on Jesus, a devoted servant who honored God by saying yes to the will of God. She was faithful to her role that would bring light to the world. She was willing to endure the shame and the nega-tive chatter about her. But despite it all, she did not back down from her assignment. In life, we must realize there is always a bigger plan than what we are going through.

Elizabeth: Mother of John the Baptist: Elizabeth, another barren woman in the Bible, was singled out by God for a special honor. When God caused her to conceive at an old age, her son grew up to become John the Baptist, the mighty prophet who heralded the coming of the Messiah. Elizabeth's story is much like Hannah's; her faith was just as strong.

Through her steadfast belief in God's goodness, she played a role in God's plan of salvation. Elizabeth teaches us God can step into a hopeless situa-tion and turn it upside down in an instant. He makes all things good in our lives. I believe that Elizabeth realized that she was a part of a bigger plan. She was a woman of great faith and courage.

Deborah played a unique role in Israel's history, serving as the only female Judge in a lawless period before the country got its first king. In this male-dominated culture, she enlisted the help of a mighty warrior named Barak to defeat the oppressive general Sisera.

Deborah's wisdom and faith in God inspired the people. Thanks to her leadership, Israel enjoyed peace for 40 years. According to the book of judges, Deborah was a prophetess of the God of the Israelites, and she was the fourth Judge of pre-monarchic Israel and the only female Judge men-tioned in the Bible. This speaks volumes of what God thought of her. I be-lieve she has set the tone for others coming behind her for generations to come.

Ruth was a virtuous young widow, so upright in character that her love sto-ry is one of the favorite accounts in the entire Bible. When her Jewish mother-in-law Naomi returned to Israel from Moab after a famine, Ruth pledged to follow Naomi and worship her God.

Boaz exercised his right as kinsman-redeemer, married Ruth, and rescued both women from poverty. According to Matthew, Ruth was the grand-mother of King David, whose descendant was Jesus Christ.

Ruth was faithful to her mother-in-law Naomi; I believe it was in her DNA to be faithful. Because of her faithfulness, God gave her favor with Boaz. We can learn a lesson from Ruth on the importance of being loyal to one another; keeping our word is so important.

Scripture: John 11:40 Then Jesus said, "Did I not tell you that if you be-lieve, you will see the glory of God?"

Do you have faith in your abilities?

Do you consider yourself a woman of great faith?

What do you like about these great women of faith?

What do you love about the story of Queen Vashti

WHAT HAPPENS WHEN FEAR COMES KNOCKING ON YOUR DOOR? FAITH ANSWERED AND SAID NO ONE IS HOME!

by Dr. Nora Shariff-Borden

I love this title; it puts a smile on my face when I read it! It shows me how powerful, relentless, and confident Faith is. She walks in her power every second of the day; she shows us what it means to trust the journey God is taking us on.

Fear has no choice but to back down when Faith shows up on the scene. She makes Fear and her best friends - doubt, insecurity, low self-esteem, unworthiness, lack of confidence, broke, lack of love of self - run the other way. Faith brings confidence, worthiness, wealth, love, and power when she walks into the room. Her presence brings a ray of light that makes your future so bright you need sunglasses. She has been a beacon of light in my life when I have sometimes felt dim. She showed up and shined her light. She made me look at my situation and realize that all things are possible for me if I would just believe. Fear knows that she can't show up in the same place as Faith.

We can have Faith in God and His plans for us, but when we get caught in the world's struggles with our very human fears, that leads nowhere. Our fears are our insecurities, our lack of Faith, our lack of belief, our self-doubt, and the list can go on and on. If Fear is at your core, ask God to give you His Faith which will shock your core of Fear. Decide today that you are going to go on a faith journey with God. Once you make that decision, you will be amazed at what will happen. I want to challenge you today to make a commitment to take the faith journey.

In Brian Moran and Michael Lennington's book, The 12-week Year, they talk about the word commitment. Commitment is a personal promise that you make to yourself. Keeping your promises to others builds strong relationships, and keeping promises to yourself builds character, esteem, and success. It is important that we become women of Faith which speaks volumes about who we are. It shows people who we are as a woman of great Faith.

I read this the other day. Faith is grounded in truth; Fear is grounded in lies. Faith is based on the promises of God. Fear is based on the deceptive lies of Satan. Faith comes by hearing the Word of God; Fear comes by hearing the lies of Satan. The next time Fear comes knocking at your door, make sure you let Faith answer the door. She will tell Fear no one is Home. I believe she says to fear "and don't come back!!!"

When we are afraid, God hears us. And He tells us to keep the Faith. Proverbs 29:25 says, "Fear of man will prove to be a snare, but whoever trusts in the Lord is kept safe." It is awesome to know that our Faith in the Lord will be our shield.

Hebrews 13:6 tells us to let our Faith be bigger than our Fear. When we allow our Faith to be a part of everything we do, it is so much easier not to allow Fear to occupy our thoughts. Here God is letting us know the importance of knowing that our Faith is bigger.

Isaiah 41:10 - Fear not, for I am with you; Be not dismayed, for I am your God. I will strengthen you, yes, I will help you, I will uphold you with my righteous right hand. The Bible tells us that God wants us to have Faith that He is with us. He is our protector, giver, and joy; the key to this all is having Faith in Him and not in Fear.

Genesis 28:15 - Behold, I am with you and will keep you wherever you go and will bring you back to this land; for I will not leave you until I have done what I have spoken to you."

Here again, we can have Faith in the power of God. He is always reassuring us that He is with us. He is letting us know that He will fulfill every promise He has spoken to us. That right there is mind-blowing to me.

I read this from Sword of the Spirit Ministries: Just as FAITH activates the hand and promises of God, FEAR can throw the principle of FAITH INTO REVERSE! When you "believe in" something other than what God has said or promised through His Word, you probably won't receive it.
By focusing on the problem(s) and the "what ifs" more than the solution, which is Christ Jesus, we will manifest the same belief system of FAITH, just in reverse. The reversal of the biblical principle of FAITH then creates emotions and images of an uncertain future. Those emotions and images that we find ourselves "believing" create the opposite of FAITH in GOD. It causes us to doubt if God can, in fact, help us, heal us, or whatever we are seeking Him for. Fear is false evidence appearing too real:

The kingdom of darkness is aware of this one principle. Nothing pleases God more than mankind, particularly his children believing and trusting in Him. That is the key!

Hebrews 11:6 - And it is impossible to please God without Faith. Anyone who wants to come to Him must believe that God exists and that He rewards those who sincerely seek him.

The Bible is full of scriptures that encourage us to have FAITH IN GOD. Our flesh wants to embrace the unknown, which is FEAR.

We must fill our spirit and mind with the word of God; it will nourish and feed our FAITH. YOU HAVE THE POWER TO CHOOSE!

FAITH OR FEAR is not something that just "happens" to us without our input. FEAR simply fills the space where FAITH should abide and takes advantage of the fact that we have NOT made a choice to have FAITH in God. I know from my own personal experiences the importance of trusting in the power of God. So, the next time Fear knocks on your door, let him know that Faith said no one is Home.

We are nothing without you, Lord, but by Your Faith, we are everything. Through Faith, our lives can be changed. When we think by Faith, it allows us to have Faith in others, Faith in ourselves, and Faith in life. The Bible teaches us, "all things are possible to her that believe" Mark 9:23 If you have Faith, nothing shall be impossible unto you" Matthew 17:20 "According to your faith be it unto you" Matthew 9:29
Bottom line: Faith Make Things Happen in Life!

Scripture:
Jeremiah 29:11 For I know the plans that I have for you, declares the LORD, plans to prosper not to harm you, plans to give you hope and a future. NIV

Do you trust that God has plans for you?

Are you executing your Faith daily?

Do you find yourself focusing more on your fears than your Faith?

Do you believe that when you are fearful that God hears you and that He will answer you?

AMBASSADOR DR. JACQUELINE MOHAIR

Bridging Gaps and Changing Lives!

Ambassador Dr. Jacqueline Mohair is a nationally known Transformational Business & Life Strategist, Advocate, Professor, Life Coach, Minister, Serial Entrepreneur, and Ambassador to the UN. In addition, she is an author who has written inspirational books on empowerment and entrepreneurship, teaching Women from all walks of life how to win through faith.

Ambassador Dr. Mohair is a premiere Life Coach helping women to turn their passion into profits and dreams into reality. An advocate for change who is passionate about empowering people to succeed in life and business, teaching humanity how to birth vision and turn their pain into purpose. Her motto is "You were created by a creator who's given you the Power to Create from the Well Within."

Contact Information:
www.jacquelinemohair.com
Themohairs@gmail.com

HOW TO FIGHT THE GOOD FIGHT OF FAITH

by Dr. Jacqueline Mohair

We lack knowledge of what God's Word says about our redemption, and that lack of knowledge is the greatest enemy of faith. Lack of knowledge of God's Word produces unbelief. Because we don't understand what Jesus did for us truly on the cross —what it means and the benefits it provides the believer—our faith is hindered.

2 CORINTHIANS 5:17
17 Therefore if any man be in Christ, He is a new creature: old things are passed away; behold, all things are become new.

Second Corinthians 5:17 is a tremendous verse of Scripture. What tremendous truths are contained in it: "... if any man be in Christ, he is a new creature...." The margin of the King James Version reads, "a new creation." Praise God, I'm glad I am a new creature—a new creation!

We Are Created in the Likeness of God

We must realize we are created in the likeness of God. The word also says that we must worship him in spirit and truth. Therefore, our spirit is speaking of the in-ward man—the real man—not speaking of the outward man. Remember, Paul said "... though our outward man perish, yet the inward man is renewed day by day" (2 Cor. 4:16). The inward man is the real you. No one can ever know himself, much less anyone else, unless he has been born again and has become a new man in Christ. Without being born again a man does not even know he is a spirit man.

According to research, many people go to a psychiatrist for someone to "under-stand" them. But a psychiatrist, unless he is a Christian psychiatrist, can never un-derstand you, because only a Christian would realize that man is a spirit being. Psychiatry has to do with the operation of the mind and emotions through the physical senses. Psychiatry operates on the assumption that man is just a body and a mind (or soul).

There are several stories of individuals that commit suicide for many different rea-sons. However, I'm told of a story of a leading psychiatrist in California had committed suicide. He was a comparatively young man, only 46. Some of the leading Hollywood movie stars had been under his care. No one could understand why this man, who seemingly had everything, would commit suicide. He lived in a beautiful, palatial home that was completely paid for. He had a large bank ac-count and no financial troubles. He had no domestic troubles. He had no physical troubles. After the last article was run, they still didn't know why he did it. Here was a man who was supposed to help others, but evidently, he didn't have the an-swer even for himself. The trouble with many people is, they are always looking at things from the physical or natural viewpoint rather than from the spiritual viewpoint. The answer to man's need exists in the spiritual realm. A man doesn't really know or understand himself unless he is a Christian, and a man who isn't a Christian is liable to do or think anything. This is because the spiritual nature of man is a fallen nature, and man cannot change his own nature. The Bible says, "Can the Ethiopian change his skin, or the leopard his spots?" (Jer. 13:23). No, man cannot change his own nature—but God can "Therefore, if any man be in Christ, he is a new creature" The inward man—the real man—is a new creation. This new creation takes on the very life and nature of God.

The outward man, however, is not a new creation. We do not receive new bodies when we are born again. The Bible says we will have a new body one day, but we don't have one yet. Meanwhile, however, the man on the inside—the real you, the spirit man—has already become a new man in Christ.

Understanding Increases Faith. I got a hold of Second Corinthians 5:17 some years ago on the bed of sickness. At that time, medical science said I could not have kids and today I have 3 and later I was diagnosed with a brain tumor. I had heard salvation preached all my life. Although I had joined a church, I had never really been born again. Yet when I prayed to receive Salvation at a church in Jackson, MS. I believed. I had no doubt in my mind that the Lord heard me. I had no lack of understanding along that line; therefore, I had no unbelief. I received salvation, and I knew I was saved or born again. Shortly, after moving to Dallas, TX and joining the Potter's House under Bishop Jakes the word became life. I remember when I joined the Potter's House, Bishop was teaching on the book of Romans. The word was opening my eyes to experience God for myself and not go by others' experience. Later, after moving to Georgia studying under Dr. Juanita Bynum, Dr. Janice Crenshaw and Dr. Sonnie Badu I experienced the Supernatural. Around the year of 2018 doctors diagnosed me with a brain tumor but God had the last say so. Today, I'm walking in my healing! He still heals today! I can go on and on about faith and his supernatural healing. I didn't know the Lord as a healer. I certainly didn't understand God's Word concerning healing for my body. We hadn't had much teaching along that line in my church's early years. About all we had heard was, "Just leave it to the Lord. After all, He knows best."(But in His Word, God has made provision for us to have His best. Praise God, He has told us how to get the best—but now it is up to us to receive what God has already provided.)

You can see how a lack of knowledge of God's Word and of our provisions in Christ can hinder faith. It hindered my faith. In time, after much study of the Word, I saw the exact steps to take in prayer and just how to release my faith to receive healing. If I had known and understood that months before, I could have been off that bed long before I was.

God didn't have a certain "set time" to come by and heal me. It wasn't until I took my eyes off my problems and started to focus on his assignment for my life that I was healed. Because God is the same every day! The trouble wasn't with God; the trouble was with me. It was my lack of knowledge of God's Word which hindered my faith. As soon as I found out what God's Word said and acted on it, I got re-sults! We cannot act upon God's Word beyond our knowledge of His Word.

Faith grows with understanding God's Word. If your faith is not growing, your knowledge of God's Word is not growing. If my faith were not growing, I would begin to ask myself why. Then I would begin to feed my faith on God's Word. If you are not growing in faith, you are not developing spiritually. My understand-ing of 2 Corinthians 5:17 made this Scripture one of my favorite verses.

I just want to leave you with a few of my favorite scriptures to help you fight this good fight of faith.

1 Timothy 6:12
Fight the good fight of faith, lay hold on eternal life, to which you were also called and have confessed the good confession in the presence of many witnesses.

Fight
Fight - this means we are in spiritual conflict.

Fight - this means there are enemies that we fight against. We know we fight against demonic powers. Paul also identifies earlier in 1 Timothy 6, that there are false doctrines that we need to stand up against.

Fight - this also means that there are weapons God has given us which we must know how to use and use them - God's Word, the name of Jesus, our authority, our faith, dependence on the Holy Spirit and so on. We must know how to fight. Sometimes we want a nice warm, cozy Christian life. But the Christian life is a 'fight' and we have no choice but to engage.

Battle Weary

Sometimes it is possible that we can get tired of fighting - we get weary. When the battle is long, drawn out. So, we need to learn to rest, refresh and renew our-selves in the Lord. (Isaiah 40:28-30)
We also need to learn to be there for each other in spiritual battle.

Good Fight

Good, as in being valuable, of value. It is a good fight because this is a fight worth fighting. It is a good fight because this is a fight which we know we are go-ing to win (2Corinthians 2:14).

Faith

This fight has to do with our faith.
The enemies are working at destroying our faith. That is what they are after.

They want to rob us of what we believe. Their weapons are designed to destroy our faith. It is also a fight we fight with our faith. We resist the enemy standing steadfast in the faith. (1 Peter 5:8,9; Ephesians 6:17).

Lay hold on eternal life

This is interesting. Eternal life is something (a) given to us freely by God (Ro-mans 6:23) and (b) something we already have - He who has the Son has life (1 John 5:11,12)..and yet we are told to "lay hold on", meaning to seize, take hold of.

Eternal life is freely given to us by God. We are already possessors of eternal life...and yet we need to fight the good fight of faith to lay hold of this and keep it in our possession.

This is true of every other blessing that God gives to us. Every blessing from heaven is freely given to us and we are already possessors of every blessing (Ephesians 1:3) ....and yet we must fight the good fight of faith to lay hold of these, make them ours and keep them in our possession. We have been called to be possessors of eternal life, called to be possessors of the blessings of God. I be-lieve if Christians will find out who they are and what they are in Christ, they will rise to the level of what belongs to them!

The trouble is, however, that some people are looking at things from the natural — from a physical standpoint. God is looking at things from a spiritual standpoint. But some Christians keep looking at themselves from the physical and they see this world of darkness and, consequently, they walk by sight and not by faith. They think defeat, they talk defeat, and then they are defeated! And they sing those old unbelieving songs such as, "Here I wander like a beggar through the heat and through the cold." These are the things that defeat Christians. As a man thinks so is he! Find out what the Bible says and begin to confess, "This is what I am in God. This is who I am in Christ." You see, I do not believe that Christ is ill. There should not be any illness in His Body! I don't believe that Jesus is defeated or that He is a failure. I believe that He is a conqueror! And that is why the Bible says, ". . . we are more than conquerors through him that loved us."

(Rom. 8:37). Let this mind that's in Christ be also in us. How do we get this mind? Simple, by studying the word and allowing the word to penetrate our mind and flow to the heart. The word says that out of the abundance of the heart the mouth speaks!

I challenge you to step out on faith and walk in the full abundance of his word for it will not return void.

I am so glad I have learned to fight the good fight of faith.

DR. RENEE HUFFMAN

Dr.(HC) Renee Huffman is a number #1 bestselling author who was born and raised in San Diego, California, to Carl and Betty Jackson. Renee Huffman has over 18 plus years of proven experience in the Financial, Mortgage, Healthcare, and Telecommunication Industries, where she has expertise in working with Fortune 500 companies such as AT&T, ING, BOEING, and ExxonMobil.

Mrs. Huffman established Dressed N' Dignity as a nonprofit organization in the fall of 2017. Our mission statement is to restore and empower women to walk in excellence in business, community, and family life by providing adequate business attire, communication skills, and necessary etiquette training.

In 2020 Renee became the owner and publisher of Women of Dignity Magazine, which focuses on telling the stories of incredible women who are impacting their local, national, and global communities. In 2021 Renee was appointed as a U.S. Delegate for Dubai connected with The Economic Hub.

Contact Information:
FB: Renee Huffman
FB Business Page: Women of Dignity Media
IG: DressedNDignity

YOUR FAITH MUST STAND TRIAL!

by Dr. Renee Huffman

What is Faith? According to the word of God Hebrews 11:1 KJV Now faith is the substance of things hoped for, the evidence of things not seen.

In Sept 2019, I decided to step away from my corporate job after almost 20 years. A Prophetess of God spoke into my life the following: "God said, "Don't go Back to Egypt".

At that moment I started to think about so many different things especially my husband of 19 years because we needed a two-household income. But I remember God was commanding and giving me instructions on letting go of the former years and behold I will do something new for your great future. Isaiah 43:18-19 KJV 18, "Remember ye, not the former things, neither consider the things of old. 19 Behold, I will do a new thing; now it shall spring forth; shall ye not know it? I will even make a way in the wilderness, and rivers in the desert."

I decided to move forward and started my first business Ms. Dignity Style & Grace which is an online boutique. I started my research looking for vendors and I found a vendor that housed millions of clothing. I was so excited and was ready to purchase my first bulk order. But the vendor's representative I was assigned to gave me a hard time and didn't want to serve me. When you have faith you will go through a lot of obstacles, trials, and challenges in your life, but this taught me how to depend on and trust God like never before. One of my favorite scriptures is Isaiah 26:3 KJV "Thou wilt keep him in perfect peace, whose mind is stayed on thee: because He trusteth in thee." It's so important to trust God when you can't see your future - this is Faith.

I assumed because I went through a lot for 20 years in corporate America that this new boutique business would take off right away, but it didn't. I found myself struggling financially but trusting God. I decided to keep showing up and eventually I was switched to another representative. The new representative was very helpful, and my boutique sales began to grow. Never be scared to speak up for yourself it could make all the difference in your business and sales.

When I think of Faith, I think of a winding road that has a lot of curves within the road, but you can't see what's ahead. I believe God gives us glimpses of our future but not our entire outcome because if you saw the in-between, you would run back to Egypt like the Israelites. I started my business officially in Oct 2019 and by Feb of 2020 I only had 4 months within the business, but it was getting harder instead of easier. I cried out to God and asked for God to give me great directions because I didn't have the answers. This is when I knew my faith was standing trial. I want you to remember the winding road.

In August 2019 (before I left corporate America), I was approached by a prestigious Christian Magazine company, that wanted to do a feature on my nonprofit organization Dressed N Dignity. I submitted my information, and the issue was released Dec 2019. God gave me favor with the editor and she gave me a job recruiting women who were making an impact in their local communities. I exceeded within that position, but it was commission based. One day I had a light bulb moment, and I could hear the voice of the Lord saying unto me, "Start your own Magazine."

I started and created Women of Dignity Magazine in 2020 right before the corona virus - a world pandemic which I didn't see coming. The business was booming, and I was on my way.

One year later my mom called and stated, "I'm not doing well, and I don't know what's wrong". I decided to go to California and help my mother, but when I got there, I had to admit her into the hospital. It wasn't looking good for her due to her oxygen levels were very low. I had never experienced this in my life. I thought I would go to California and help my mother and be back to my business in Texas. I ended up being in California for 30 days and I became my mother's caregiver. She was told she had a heart failure. This meant my mother would need 24-hour care. Here I go again, my faith was being tested and on trial. I had to lean on my faith in God, for him to show me how to run my business out of town and assist my mother. I had to stand on my Faith, and trust God like never before.

Here are a few things I did during those times when my faith was on trial. I want to recommend you do them while standing on faith:
- Trust
- Depend solely on God
- Pray
- Fear Not
- Meditate
- Lean on God

When you decide to walk by faith and not by sight you must read the word of God daily to understand the meaning of walking by faith. The Bible has given us great examples of men and women who faced many trails, but they walked by faith. The scripture also speaks of those great clouds of witnesses who are cheering us on according to Heb 12:1 KJV, "Therefore, since we are surrounded by such a huge crowd of witnesses to the life of faith, let us strip off every weight that slows us down, especially the sin that so easily trips us up. And let us run with endurance the race God has set before us."

You must have a made-up mind to walk with God. Every day will not be a bed of roses, but it will be a bed of thrones, that will cause you to navigate to your next level.

In my closing, one of my favorite characters in the Bible is Enoch. He trusted and walked by faith with God every day. God was so impressed my Enoch's Faith; He took him to heaven and man didn't see him anymore. This is the key to Faith we must fellowship with God daily. When we do, the winding road (curves of the road) will no longer frighten us, but it will allow us to walk with great patience, trust, and strength and know that the Lord will see us through any situation we face.

Lord thank you for teaching me how to stand firm in my faith while it is on trial!

CHERYL
MORGAN WILSON

Cheryl, also referred to as Coach Morgan, is a transformational coach. As a result of her efforts, clients have experienced transformational breakthroughs. By understanding their Why, Team Leaders have conquered their transitions and empowered their teams. As a professional storyteller, Coach Morgan has helped her clients improve their communication abilities. Her clients have also learned PPE (plan-prepare-execute), which offers them clarity in their pursuit of greater life success.

With extensive experience as a College Professor, Transformational and Inspirational Speaker, and Youth Leader. Cheryl has influenced the education of numerous individuals by assisting them in being purposeful, strategic, and productive. Cheryl is an excellent listener and problem-solver; she can help you find solutions to your issues. In addition, she is the CEO of her own company. "I AM LIFE 4 U Academy, LLC.

She seeks clients who desire sustainable transformation. Whom do you know?

Contact Information:
iamlife4u@gmail.com
IAMCOACHMORGAN.COM
(623) 210-0770

FAITH WILL HELP YOU ENDURE YOUR TRIALS IN LIFE

by Cheryl Morgan Wilson

"Consider it pure joy, my brothers, and sisters, whenever you face trials of many kinds. Because you know that the testing of your faith produces perseverance." - James 1:3

In 2017 I received a call. That my son had taken his life and two others. He was only 33 years old and had his whole life ahead of him, yet this tragedy happened suddenly.

It was a sunny Saturday morning. I was all alone in the church setting up for a wedding. I received a call that would change my life forever. It was a call that no parent wants to get. I was told that my son was possibly in a shooting incident. This was very strange and unusual behavior for him, and for me to hear this was shocking and unbelievable. I asked her to call me back when she was certain of the news. After I hung up from her, I said to the Lord he is not my son he belongs to you. I don't know what's going on, but you do Lord. I trust you; I trust you.

Then I started praising God and dancing around the church. I fell to the floor and started praying to thank God for being in control of the situation and letting Satan know that this was war, and he was not going to ruin this wedding or me. I then received a phone call from one of the ministers from Boston that the news was on the internet. I hung up and started calling my family members because I did not want them to hear it on the news. I decided to keep setting up for the wedding. After I finished setting up the church, I went home, got dressed, and came back to the wedding.

While I was there. I received numerous calls from my son's friends and college mates. Then I received a call from a detective confirming my son was the shooter and he had shot himself in the head and was dead. I responded by asking what I needed to do next, and he informed me that I would be getting a call from the Miami police department. At this point I felt like Job. God used me to call my siblings and my son's dad and other family members to tell them of the tragedy.

I decided to stay for the wedding. I even went to the reception because I just believed that I needed to show and tell God that when I said I trusted him, I trusted him. When I said that my son did not belong to me, he did not belong to me. He belonged to you. I wanted my mother to know, but I did not want to tell her on the telephone. I wanted my pastors in Boston to go to her house and tell her with my sisters that her grandson was dead.

Does this sound unbelievable to you? It was truly an unbelievable situation that caught us all by surprise. So much so that my son's dad stressed over his son's death, had a heart attack, and died four days later. My thoughts were "Is this happening, is this a divine disruption? I remember shaking my head at times to say this can't be real. With the realization that I was going to have to handle this alone since my ex-husband had died, I didn't have time to grieve. With the help of my sisters and my son's friends, we were able to move his body back to Boston and clear out his apartment.

There are many things that I learned from my son's death: that life is so unpredictable. As the Bible states, "tomorrow is not promised to any of us." Tomorrow will always come but will you be in it? I had two funerals - one in Boston and one in Miami. Through my son's unexpected death some have even come to Christ! "Where oh death, is your victory? Where oh death is your sting" 1corinthians 15:55

After reading this you might be asking yourself how did she endure this tragedy? I endured through the belief in Christ and his promise that He would never leave me nor forsake me. Through faith in God, I expected his favor to follow me everywhere I went, His love to sustain me, and His promises to keep me focused. However, the loss of my son has taken some of the faith wind out of my sail. I was broken, bruised and at times I was confused. Why did God take my only child and why did I feel like Job? Was God testing me or did he allow Satan to try me? I was mad at times but not at God - at my son for his actions. He used to say to me mummy we are all we've got; let's always have each other's back. I truly feel like my son let me down. He's not here to see me grow old gracefully, he didn't leave me with a daughter-in-law or any grandchildren. Why did God allow this to happen? God's answer to me was "did I give you your son to replace me"? No, He didn't. So, I used my faith to help me live which was a choice I made.

Through many life changes, people will often choose to let themselves go or deal with the trials in a non-beneficial way. 1 Corinthians 10:23 "Everything is permissible for me" but not everything is beneficial. So, in my trial, I chose to do what was most beneficial to me, but at times that was very hard to do. First, I chose to forgive, then I chose to live, then I chose to give to others who were going through their rough times. This type of movement was therapy for me. It helped me take my mind off my pain. I had to learn how to not park in my pain. This can be a challenge. With every challenge, I looked for opportunities to serve others and myself. Serving yourself is very important in life. My faith in God helped me to learn how to let go and move forward remembering that He is my source of everything.

Peace, love, joy, patience, forgiveness, but the greatest of these is Love. First love for God, self, and others. 1 Peter 4:8 Above all, love one another deeply because love covers over a multitude of sins. Your faith starts like a small mustard seed and it's your duty to plant it and nourish it to grow. Faith without works is dead or useless. Faith must be watered, pruned, spoken, and believed. Without these things, your faith will lay dormant and ineffective in your life. Your faith is like a muscle; you must train it to be strong, you must work it to see it and you must believe it to receive it. Faith is the currency that pleases God.

In closing, let us remember that faith is stronger than fear, it's strong faith that helps you endure life's trials. Faith is not without a fight so put on your armor and know that your trials are only temporary. You have already won.

But thanks be to God! He gives us victory through our Lord Jesus Christ. Therefore, my dear brothers and sisters, stand firm, let nothing move you. Always give yourselves fully to the work of the Lord because you know that your labor in the Lord is not in vain.

I am so glad that my faith has helped me to endure the trials in my life!

OUR TIMES ARE IN GOD'S HANDS!

REV. DR. STEPHANIE CASTRO

Rev. Dr. Stephanie Castro is a Senior Sales Director with a direct selling company, a Transformation Instructional Coach with the Boston Public Schools, and an ordained Itinerant Elder in the African Methodist Episcopal Church. Stephanie's people-building skills, interactive training, and inspirational messages have landed her in a position where she can now enrich the lives of those she is blessed to impact.

A graduate of the University of Bridgeport and Payne Theological Seminary, Rev. Castro has utilized her education in marketing and education to grow a business that combines her teaching skills with her experience as an ordained minister to create an atmosphere of growth and joy for all who enter. She and her husband, Rev. Pedro A. Castro, Jr., currently serve as a team at Grant A.M.E. Church in Boston. They have enjoyed a thriving ministry from the Island of Bermuda to Syracuse, NY, and now Boston over the past 16 years. Their Marketplace Ministry approach has impacted the masses as they continue to strive for excellence. They share a blended family of 3: Chantelle, Jasmyn, and Khaivon, and one grandson, Camren.

Contact Information:
pinkladysteff@gmail.com
IG: @pinkladysteff
(617) 396-0852

GOD WILL USE YOUR TRIALS TO STRENGTHEN YOUR FAITH

by Rev. Dr. Stephanie Castro

When I was diagnosed with triple negative breast cancer in March of 2021, I immediately felt that the Lord wanted me to share my journey with others. I felt that it would be the best way for me to cope with the challenges to come. By sharing my journey on social media, I have been able to impact many people who are either survivors or thrivers. Social media was one way to share, but I also felt a strong calling to write a book. I really wanted a medium where I could share with others who were also going through similar experiences to let them know that there is hope, and there is a way to keep your joy through rough times. Being able to share as a contributor to this powerful anthology, however, is yet another way to demonstrate to others the power of faith and how it can help them through the many trials of their life.

It seems like yesterday that I received a call from my doctor letting me know that the cells in my breast and under my arm were in fact cancer. It was like I already knew what he was going to say. Two days later I received another call that my blood sugar was 458 and that I had type 2 diabetes. That was one I didn't see coming. I knew I had an uphill journey at this point. Nevertheless, I also knew that I was facing a situation with a spirit of joy and a measure of faith that would ultimately be tested. I could see clearly that this would be a trial that God would use to strengthen my faith and elevate my joy at the same time.

There is a way to discover joy during the good times and bad times, and to ultimately know that joy is not something that the world can give, but it is something that comes from within. God's faithfulness during a trial has joy incorporated throughout the process. I found that my faith in God continues to keep me during this current season in my life. When none of the 15 rounds of chemotherapy were effective on this dreaded tumor, my faith was strengthened. When surgery was no longer an option, my faith was tested. When the cancer cells traveled to my lung area, my faith was strengthened. When they said the cancer was no longer curable only controllable, my faith was strengthened. Now that chemotherapy is a lifelong treatment, my faith was strengthened.

There are experiences in life that will strengthen your faith and test your joy. However, it's the confidence of knowing that everything will be alright that gets you through. Joy is everlasting because it comes from the One who is lasting.

It's no coincidence that my blood type is O-positive! I have always said that cancer messed with the wrong boobs because my positive energy is no match for cancer. Positivity is a state of mind that resides within. What I have found for myself is that positivity is a gift. My purpose in life is to bring joy to other people. When I enter a space, the space is immediately brightened. People often tell me that I make everything bright. For me, that light comes from my belief in a higher power. I am an ordained clergy woman in the African Methodist Episcopal Church. Growing up in the church, I was exposed to people who endured serious issues and were successful at getting through. That has always been my example of how joy remains despite circumstances. This joy has been another wonderful asset that has helped to strengthen my faith during this trial.

I am reminded of a Saturday during intercessory prayer where I finally understood my purpose. My husband had prepared tent cards with different prayer concerns on each one, and they were placed on the back of the pews at the church; we would stand in front of each card and pray silently for that particular concern. I was at a point in my life where I was doing so many different things, but I wasn't fulfilling anything that I was engaged in - being a mom, teacher, wife, or working in direct sales. I was not feeling fulfilled completely in any one of those areas in which I was engaged.

One of the cards said, Understand and Know God's Purpose for Your Life. I thought to myself, what is my purpose? What is the common thread in everything that I do? The answer is that I give joy and positive energy in everything I do. I bring joy to every situation or experience that I engage with others. This was God speaking to my spirit and confirming my purpose. God called me to be an Ambassador of Joy, and I embrace that responsibility fully. Bring joy to my people!!! I am so glad that I don't look like what I'm going through or what I've been through and that has a lot to do with my frame of mind. My natural state is joy and positive energy. I am an energy giver, but I need energy to thrive. I can't thrive in a negative environment. It's not uncommon for me to speak up when I'm in a negative space. If we spend a lot of time harping on what is terrible or what is wrong, the possibilities become clouded.

Focus on what you do have instead of obsessing over what you don't have. I believe everyone has a purpose for being here on earth. This joy I have, for example, the world didn't give it to me, and the world can't take it away.

What do joy and faith have in common? They both come from God. God gives us all a measure of faith that allows us to deal with life's greatest and most difficult challenges. You see faith is the substance of things hoped for and the evidence of things not seen. It takes both faith and joy to get through trials. Faith because we don't know the outcome of the situation ahead of time, and joy because we know that we know God's got it. We need faith because it gives us hope in the thing we don't yet see, and we need joy to help us cope with the many feelings we will experience during the trial.

How do we discover joy on the mountain and in the valley? It takes an unwavering faith in a God that will never disappoint. It takes an inner conviction that no matter the circumstance, you know you will come out of this better than you were going in. It takes a steadfast, unmovable love for God with a bold declaration that your joy is everlasting because it comes from the One who is lasting. That's what it takes to discover joy in all of life's topsy turvy, ups and downs, and curve balls it will undoubtedly throw when least expected. That's what it takes to stare your dire circumstance in the face and declare that by His stripes you are healed. And declare that greater is He that is in you than he that is in the world. And declare that He knows the plans He has for you. And declare your hope is built on nothing less than Jesus' blood and righteousness. And declare, I shall live and not die!

Joy is that thing you can access at any time. Because it comes from God and God alone, it is not something that will try to elude you. Sometimes it will take some effort to access that moment that triggers a memory that will remind you of the joy you already have inside of you.

Remember what it feels like to be in a place of joy: when things are going well in your church, your home, your life, your family, your office, remember that feeling, and hold on to that memory. When things are going awry, access that joyful memory of when things were going great! All in all, focus on the joy and your faith will continue to strengthen with every experience. Faith and joy are close cousins that will get you through any trial you may face. I am certain that with both concepts working in tandem, God knew exactly what would bring us to and through the trials of life. I believe that this is just one of many trials I will have to face, but I am also convinced that God is faithful to me, and He will bring me through as His walking miracle of joy!

I am thankful that He has used my trials to strengthen my faith!

DR. HARRIET ROBERSON

TV Personality, Motivational/Inspirational Speaker, Networking Strategist, International Best Selling Author, Entrepreneur, Philanthropist.

Known as the Kingdom Connector, Dr. Harriet is the Co-Founder of WEN (Women's Empowerment Network), Great Marriages Rock, and ImpactHer Women's Fellowship. Dr. Harriet is also a Speaker Trainer with the National Association of Minority Speakers. In addition, she is the recipient of the 2022 Presidential Lifetime Achievement Award and serves on numerous boards.

Dr. Harriet is married to her husband of 41 years, and together, they have two married daughters, a son, and two grandsons.

Contact Information:
www.HarrietRoberson.com
FB/Twitter/IG: @harrietroberson

MY FAITH SAYS LORD I TRUST YOU

by Dr. Harriet Roberson

Oxford Language Dictionary defines Trust as a firm belief in the reliability, truth, ability, or strength of someone or something.

The same dictionary defines Faith as the complete Trust or confidence in someone or something.

The religious definition of Faith is a strong belief in God or in the doctrines of a religion based on spiritual apprehension rather than proof.

The biblical definition of Faith comes from Hebrews 11:1 (NLT) "Faith shows the reality of what we hope for; it is the evidence of things we cannot see."

This function of Faith is about the covenant of God, which is called Faith. The Bible says, "Be strong and courageous! Do not be afraid, and do not panic before them. For the LORD, your God, will personally go ahead of you. He will neither fail you nor abandon you." Deuteronomy 31:6 (NLT)

In our walk with God, we must have Faith and Trust in the Lord with everything in us. We must be steadfast and unmovable and use our Faith to remind us that just what God said in his word, He will never leave us, fail us, or abandon us.

So often, the enemy sends trials, tribulations, issues, and situations to shake our Faith and Trust in God.

Many times, in my life, I have had to use my Faith to trust the Lord despite what the circumstances looked like or even what it felt like. I had to remind myself, "For we walk by faith, not by sight." (2nd Corinthians 5:7 NLT) Although I could not see or sometimes even feel God, I used my Faith to know; He was always there.

My Faith and Trust in the Lord pulled me through many dark times in my life, even when I wondered, God, where are you in this situation? Many days as I cried, I said, God, if you love me, why would you allow me to go through so much hell in my marriage or so much hell in my family? God, why would you allow so much tragic loss of my loved ones?

My Faith and Trust in God reminded me that although we may not understand why we are going through this, we must know for ourselves what Proverbs 3:5 (NIV) says "Trust in the Lord with all your heart and lean not on your own understanding."

I had to learn to stop looking at others and what I thought was favor in their lives and wondering why I did not have the same favor or even more. After all, I am God's favorite child.

I had to trust that God was using my issue, my tribulation, to catapult me to another level of anointing, Trust, and Faith. Without that Trust and Faith, I would have given up on my marriage, and we would not be celebrating over forty-one years of marital bliss. Without Trust and Faith, I would not have overcome so many obstacles and ploys to destroy me and my ministry. Additionally, I would not have accomplished so much in my life without learning to use my Faith to trust God through it all.

On this journey of showing God my Faith and that I trust Him, I realized the importance of God's timing in my life. I had to learn to wait on God to create His timetable, His direction, and His purpose for my life.

It was my Faith and Trust that God knew what was best for me that helped me realize that if God had done what I believed was the blessing I was looking for, it could have destroyed me because it wasn't His timing. I now know God could not have fulfilled my hopes and dreams early in my life because I could not have handled the fame, fortune, and notoriety at age thirty, forty, or, truth be told, even fifty. My Faith and Trust taught me how to handle tribulations and to do what the Bible says in 1 Peter 5:7, "Give all your worries and cares to God, for he cares about you."

The enemy's job is to create doubt in your Faith, your confidence, and your Trust in God. But if you keep the mindset to take every thought captive, you can turn every negative and discouraging thought over to God. In other words, catch that negative thought and turn it around before it festers in your mind to discourage you.

On this journey, you must have the Faith that shows God, you trust Him. I encourage you to be positive, even in negative situations. Not only will you have better-coping skills in stressful situations, but your outlook on life will also be brighter and happier. Having a positive mindset will give you the strength and confidence to go through any situation, knowing it is only for a season.

When your Faith is shaken by life's ups and downs, remind yourself what Romans 8:28 (NLT) says, "And we know that God causes everything to work together for the good of those who love God and are called according to his purpose for them."

You must trust that God has got you. Even if you cannot see it, He knows what He is doing, and He is working it out for your good.

For those dealing with health issues, keep your Faith and Trust that God can completely heal you. If you have issues in your marriage, keep the Faith and Trust that God is turning that marriage around. If you are single and waiting for God to send your mate, do not get distracted by the first shiny thing that comes along. And do not get discouraged and accept less than what God has for you.

For those who are having financial issues, let your Faith and Trust in God pull you out of that situation. I suggest you start with prayer and then have the Faith to believe God can do whatever you ask Him to do.

Mathew 21:22 says, "You can pray for anything, and if you have faith, you will receive it."

Mathew 17:20 says, "You don't have enough faith," Jesus told them. "I tell you the truth, if you had faith even as small as a mustard seed, you could say to this mountain, ''Move from here to there,'' and it would move. Nothing would be impossible."

Now do not think you can manage any of that with just Faith without putting some work in. The Bible says in James 2:17 (NLT), "So you see, Faith by itself isn't enough. Unless it produces good deeds, it is dead and useless." " James 2:17 (NKJV) "Thus also faith by itself, if it does not have works, is dead." " Sometimes you need to tell God, yes, I believe in you, but I am willing to do my part as well.

If you are seeking healing, pray and seek God to lead you to the right doctor, and if needed, do your part to get healthy or get the treatments needed to be healed. To save your marriage, it may take seeing a marriage counselor. For singles, maybe see a relationship coach and make sure you are on the right track to receive your mate. For financial woes, it may take sacrifice - budgeting, getting an extra job, or finding a financial counselor. Whatever it takes, trust God, take the extra step, and by Faith, God will work it out. I once heard someone say, "Trials without God will break you, but if you have God, it will make you."

Trust the direction that God leads you. Don't be afraid; just pray and watch how God will have His way."

Remember, God is bigger than anything you will ever face in your life. Through every circumstance, when you keep the Faith and learn to trust in Jesus, you will have victory in every area of your life where your Faith and Trust are challenged.

God Loves you, and He is waiting on you to show Him that your Faith and your Trust are totally in Him.

I am so thankful that my Faith has shown God that I trust Him.

DR. ANGELA BENNETT

Angela Bennett is a 7-time #1 best-selling author, coach, and CEO and founder of Angie B Transformations, a multi-dimensional coaching specialty, centered on the complete revitalization of the lives of despondent women, taking them from powerless to POWERFUL. Seamlessly infusing personal style assessment and recreation, coupled with the facilitation of transformative life coaching, Dr. Bennett offers clients an authentic depiction of what life looks like when changed by the power of spiritual, physical, and mental edification.

Her mantra is simple: As one reshaped from the ashes of an unfortunate past, Angela exists to help women know and understand that one's past does not define them. It refines them. She pledges to reach out to those at their personal breaking points, lifting them out of the pits they find themselves in, empowering them to fall deeply and fiercely in love with themselves, and unleashing their voice and power as she has done for herself.

Contact Information:
https://linktr.ee/angieb_transformations

Note: This author is from Sydney, Australia, and therefore some words may not be spelled as they are in the American English language.

YOUR FAITH WILL TAKE YOU FROM DARKNESS TO LIGHT - DANGEROUS LIAISONS

by Dr. Angela Bennett

Steal, Kill, Destroy. The devil had his way with me.
My mind barely had fight left in it, and my body had already given over.

Addiction had somehow reasserted its stranglehold on my life. My demons' weapon of choice was alcohol, and my preferences were French Champagne and vodka. Normally celebratory, but in my hands, they made for a dangerous liaison of a cocktail. One called Catastrophe, except, I never stopped at one. The slide had not felt that dramatic, but like every slope in my life, it was slippery when wet. The truth was I knew, with each sip, that I was encouraging my demons every time I mixed their favourite bottles.

It had been years, but that didn't matter. I was in the same place all over again. All my work, my years of recovery, and my growth were reduced to memory as I lay on the shower floor again, drunk. Except for this time, I was intent on not just wallowing but ending it all. It was a new shower low. Rock bottom.

How did I get here again? Decades of disappointment, grief, and trauma overwhelmed me. A lifetime of suppressed emotions and unresolved heartache had driven me to numb my emotions, but this was razor's edge. My alcohol co-dependency had started as a life-saver, but it now reduced my mindset to that of a life-taker.

I almost lost my life at the hands of an ex-lover, and back then, I begged for mercy and ran for my life. I fought him so hard to live, and here I was, wanting to die... at my own hands.

The person who found me picked up my drunk, limp body off the shower floor, clothed and put me to bed as she watched over me, so I didn't, was my twenty-one-year-old daughter, who confided in me as I woke. "Mum, you broke me."

My little girl. Too painful to hear; the harsh reality of my addiction was finally too painful to bear.
In shady, quiet places, my addiction had been destroying my mind, my body, and my life, but now it threatened to destroy my relationship with my children.

When was enough going to be enough? When was I going to wake up to the damage I had caused?

My daughter telling me I had broken her broke me. It broke something in my psyche too. Her words, so plain and raw, had short-circuited my brain and defined a moment when enough was finally enough. The moment I knew it was up to me to make different choices. That if I changed nothing, then nothing would change.

The wake-up call was a literal one, and I started searching for help the next day. I called rehab and recovery places, one after another. I figured if I were in such a desperate place, surely these places would be desperate to let me in. Unfortunately, the costs were prohibitive, and the waitlists were long - the type of frustrating blow that would normally have me reach for a drink.

It was hard to conceive that recovery centres were asking people for so much money and then telling them to wait when the caller was asking for help so she wouldn't take her life.

One woman said the minimum would be three weeks, and it went through my head that in three weeks, I could be dead. She was clinical and transactional, so this business of me wanting to end my life would clearly have to wait or be better bankrolled. If I sold my car, the waitlist was still non-negotiable. So, I was left to wait it out on my own suicide watch. I felt like such a failure that even rehab was out of reach for me. Earmarked for the rich. And the patient. It was frustrating and sobering on a different level. So, I prayed and only persevered because I had no choice. No choice but to heal, but to confront myself and my world of hurt.

I knew, deep inside, the road to restoring my dignity would be rough, and I would need God to rely on. Though my determination was starting to feel grittier, I also knew that if I did not get a place soon and surrender my future, I would likely not have one.

I dialed the numbers quicker and got to the point faster. Sweating and nerve wrecked, I was finally accepted into an outpatient service. Relief pulsed through me. There was apprehension, but it was a first step in the direction I needed to go, which was the opposite direction to where my demons normally pulled me. But boy, was I in for a ride.

The following days were a confronting blur. Alcohol has a come-down effect, so my brain was desperate for its next dopamine hit. The cycle of addiction was not ok with my sudden, rational rehab decision, but I knew I could not give in or up.

I was scared for my life, and the fear was in my own hands this time. I had to show myself mercy, and it was starting to feel like the most courageous thing I had ever done.

I did not know how much conviction it would take, how much bravery and commitment I would need, to keep choosing to tell the truth and to come to grips with the reality of everything I had suppressed over so many years. Decades even... all dulled and numbed with alcohol and cocaine.

As I write this, I am eight months in recovery, so I have more ahead of me than I do behind me, and it has felt like dragging myself through mud most days, but prayer and visions sustain me.

One vision is of a desert – a landscape of nothingness, and yet through the dehydrated, cracked dirt, a single flower crops up. I have experienced kindness and gentleness amidst the desolation, which, like my flower, has symbolised hope to me. That a flower can be as stubborn as the rough terrain, and things can bloom even amidst the shattered pieces of my heart.

This season has been one of Sweet Surrender for me. It has required the death of the old Angela, creating space for the new Angela to rise and step into her power. Easier said than done.

I envisioned a future version of myself, but no one can prepare you for the depth of healing work that will be asked of you to become the version you truly wish to become.

By the same token, I had not realized that the version I envisioned does not scratch the surface of who I am becoming. The kernels of me that had to die and lay waste on the grounds of my past were necessary to produce seeds destined for purpose and filled with higher intentions for my life.

I felt dirty, exposed, and vulnerable through the early days of my healing. I could barely lift my head or meet another's eyes, but the exposure of all my dirt was cleansing too. Comfort came each time I asked for it.

In still moments, I heard a verse from the Song of Solomon:

Can you not discern a NEW DAY of destiny breaking forth around you?

The incessant waiting called me to discern. To clear my shame and to know instead that I am fearfully and wonderfully made, to speak my guilt and know that I am forgiven and can be washed clean.

Some days were spent on the floor crying for hours, pouring my heart out to God, but my suffering became the invitation to discern. I could choose Gratitude in the moments that cracked me wide open, Surrender amidst the turmoil I created, Growth in the depths of my anguish, and Safety in the refuge of my Father's love.

I could choose a place inside where I belonged, and I could dwell in peace as myself. Often, it is only through our despair that we surrender to Him in all our vulnerability, and our surrender births the opportunity to cultivate an unshakeable trust in God. For everything that sparkles with strength and beauty is made in the dark.

Bamboo does not see the light for years. Long after people have stopped watering it, it grows and fortifies in the dark. It finds its nourishment in the soil, and when it is ready, it shoots through the ground with a speed and strength that astounds.

God is our source and soil, and He desires us to grow and thrive, no matter how much time we have spent in darkness. He will never stop watering our dreams or desires, and He asks that we trust as bamboo does.

For 27 years, I held a dream of sharing my story of radical transformation from prostitution, domestic violence, depression, and now alcohol addiction, and suicide attempts into a life of surviving, thriving even, and victory.

God planted that dream in me, and now I understand what He planted; He will not allow it to die in me. He is bringing it to pass beyond my wildest dreams, no matter how disheartened I become or how many times I fail and want to give up or run and hide. He is determined to see His dream that He planted in me live and empower others in similar situations.

Lord Thank You for allowing my faith to take me from darkness to your marvelous light.

DR. BARBARA JACKSON

Dr. Barbara Jackson is the CEO and President of Barbara Jackson Global and BJ Financial Support Service LLC.

She's an author, community leader, certified Life Strategist Coach, Financial professional, motivational speaker, and philanthropist.

Barbara co-founded The Women's Empowerment Network (WEN) & ImpactHer 501c3 organizations. It encourages, inspires, and supports women in reaching greatness. She also contributes to the SoulSistas10x Network, which promotes ministry and businesswomen on social media.

She challenges men and women to seek their purpose and gives them skills and techniques to reach their God-given destiny. Her latest BetterME mentorship program, Destined to Reign, helps individuals discover their true calling and reshape their mindset.

She and her husband, Henry Jackson, founded Greater Life Worship Center International in Davenport, Florida.

Dr. Barbara has a Ph.D. in Humanities, MA in Organizational Leadership, and BA in Biblical Studies & Accounting. Barbara has been married to Henry Jackson, Sr., for 30 years. They have five children, Eric, Erica, Henry III, Joshua, and Hannah, plus two daughters-in-law and two sons-in-law. In addition, they have eight beautiful grandchildren. She enjoys traveling, cooking, and spending time with her grandchildren.

Contact Information:
www.barbarajacksonglobal.com
barbarajacksonglobal@gmail.com
IG: drbarbjackson
FB: Barbara Jackson
Tiktok: drbarbjackson
Twitter: mzbarb7
Clubhouse: drbarbaraj
(407) 569-6367

LEARNING HOW TO HAVE PEACE ON YOUR FAITH JOURNEY

by Dr. Barbara Jackson

It takes effort and perseverance to learn how to have peace on your spiritual journey, but when used properly, it benefits your mind, body, and soul. Whether you identify it or not, we are all on a life journey, but using biblical tools and strategies can help us achieve serenity.

Let us define the meaning of peace: calm and absence of disturbance and faith is unwavering belief or trust in someone or something. And when we look at the definition of journey as the act of moving from one location to another.

The Bible tells us, "Do not be anxious about Anything, but in every situation, by prayer and petition, with thanksgiving, present your requests to God. And the peace of God, which transcends all understanding, will guard your hearts and your minds in Christ Jesus." Philippians 4:6-7

We are encouraged through this verse to not become anxious about Anything! Some may say why would God tell us this when He knows we are fleshly beings. What we sometimes fail to notice, God always gives us a solution for getting through every situation. He tells us to pray, make our requests known and finally give thanks. When we do it in that order, it is guaranteed peace.

God desires that we live, walk, and function from a place of peace. It is at that place it requires faith must be in operation.

We live in a world where life can be inconsistent, and even though there are many curve balls, we must have an anchor to rely upon. If not, our days will be filled with anxiety and no peace or tranquility. And this goes against God's will for our lives.

If we are on this earth, there will be problems, issues, disappointment, sickness, financial woes, and family drama. However, Jesus provides a solution for us; He tells us to cast our cares upon him because He will take care for us. Now that is good news.

As a believer, there are decisions we must make as we face every circumstance in our lives. We must allow the Holy Spirit to guide us on how to manage it in the best way to get the best outcomes.

I've made a lot of bad choices in the past that didn't turn out well. Even yet, when I decided to trust God and communicate with Him in prayer for guidance and clarification, can I share with you that those were the moment a divine peace descended upon me. My burden and fear were replaced with a supernatural peace that I couldn't describe in words. This peace surpasses all my understanding.

When living in a world of chaos, we must put our faith in God from the beginning to the end. Faith is having confidence in God's ability to protect us from the enemy's grasp and deliver us from all harm.

God had already proclaimed that we are winners before we had even lived one day of our lives. If our circumstances don't match what he promised, it does not mean that we are losers. It simply means that we haven't arrived yet, so keep pushing ahead, believing, trusting God, and praying until it looks like what He promised. We serve a God that keeps all his promises.

We can't see our way out when we are in the middle of our storms. But when we remind ourselves what the Bible states, God will not leave us, nor will he forsake us. It can give us peace on our journey successfully. I can remember when I was traveling home from work. Although it appeared to be a wonderful day, the weather rapidly deteriorated. It changed right away when a sudden, heavy rain started to pour down. I could not see my front, back, right, or left sides. I worried immediately and decided to call my husband, explaining how terrible the weather was and how terrified I was. He started praying for me right away. The adversary showed a visual of me being involved in a fatal accident and dying. It was quite detailed. Before hearing the voice of God say, "Didn't, I say that I will never leave you or forsake you?" I almost believed it. Do you trust me in areas where I'm hard to find?

I instantly started to cry and shouted, "Help me, Oh God," and kept driving home, confident that He would fulfill His promise. Instead, I was reminded that the God we serve was the same one that spoke to the storms in the Bible and ordered the wind to cease blowing. Meanwhile, the wind immediately stopped, and the storms subsided. The rain ceased shortly after I finished praying; in fact, there was no rain near the city where I reside. I immediately begin to give Hm praises and glory. He was the same God working for me on those bright and sunny days as He was on stormy and dreary days. God was demonstrating His presence in both circumstances.

When we keep our eyes on Jesus and not the situation, He is the one that calms the storms in our lives. I call Him my storm calmer, so get your eyes off the storm, and keep them on the one, who calms the storm.

I want you to give reference to Elijah's story in the Bible. You'll notice in Elijah's account that the time between his act of faith and fear is only a few days. He recently ended Bael's prophets and has already witnessed fire descending from heaven. So why does he suddenly perceive this new circumstance as hopeless? Has he lost sight of the divine power that will become available in a few days? Sadly, it appears that the answer is yes. Elijah's perspective has changed, but God's influence and capacity to receive that power have not. His mentality alters everything since he is no longer focused on God's strength but rather on the terrifying situation. I, therefore, assume Elijah is unbalanced and inconsistent in his walk when I read these things.

I must say, though, that I have experienced similar emotions in my own life. It would be obvious that God's wonderful faithfulness is at work when I saw his strong hands at work on my behalf throughout my life. But then, some bizarre event would occur, sending me back into this horrible state of terror, rage, discontent, unbelief, or even doubting God. Can I say that I am so extremely appreciative of His tolerance and love for us?

However, we should remember that God honors His promises when we encounter those frightening situations when the real world does not match what He has promised. He will make certain that we triumph. We worship a powerful God who can create opportunities where none previously existed. According to the Bible, everything will work out for our benefit even when we cannot see or understand. God is especially skilled in circumstances when men assert that nothing will work and that nothing can be changed, even when we have trusted him and cannot trace him. God will forever remain faithful and true; I want you to walk into your perfect peace today that God gives you.

The Bible reminds us below of the peace that He gives. "Peace, I leave with you; my peace I give you. I do not give to you as the world gives. Do not let your hearts be troubled, and do not be afraid." John 14:27

Prayer:
Today, I choose your supernatural peace to live and abide within me. Let this peace rise and take residence within my heart. I thank you for guarding the entrance to my heart and mind, I trust you with my life, and I

will obey you when you speak. I decree and declare the enemy will not be able to affect me as he did in the past. I thank you that now my eyes are open to see, and my ears are unstopped so I can hear the enemy before he attempts to steal my joy and frustrate my spirit. Lord, we thank you that you don't give us what the world gives but that you give us your perfect peace even when things seem hard sometimes. I decree and declare perfect peace stands guard at the door of our heart. I come against the spirit of fear, frustration, and anxiety, and I declare it will not enter, but we welcome perfect peace, bountiful joy, and a sound mind. Thank You for loving me enough to give me such a strong supernatural peace in You. I pray this by faith in the name of Jesus! AMEN

Declare today that Supernatural Peace shall be my portion, so I walk in Perfect Peace in Every Area of my Life!!

I am so thankful that I have learned to have peace on my faith journey.

MEKITA
WHITFIELD

Mekita K. Whitfield is a native of Chicago, Illinois and a proud product of the public education school system. Through prayer, hard work, and faith, Mekita acquired a Bachelor of Arts in English and a Master of Science in Politics and Government from Illinois State University, Master of Arts in Secondary Education from Chicago State University and a Master of Arts in Educational Administration from the American College of Education.

She is a certified public speaker from the National Speaker's Academy and a licensed Esthetician from Dudley Beauty College in Chicago, Illinois. Mekita is a lifelong learner who believes education is the key to success. She served in education for eighteen years as an English Language Arts teacher. Currently, she is a Middle-School, Administrator. In addition to her many accomplishments, Mekita finds joy as the CEO of her organization, Phenomenal Team In Action.

She is happily married to the love of her life Dr. Lajuan Whitfield Sr., pastor of New Life Holiness Church Chicago. Their blended family consists of two beautiful children, Lajuan Jr. and Lauren, and a lovely granddaughter, Zora. Mekita's goal and mission are to enrich lives, one face at a time, as she inspires before she expires.

Contact Information:
mekitam@hotmail.com
(312) 809-0877
Facebook: Mekita K. Whitfield
Instagram: mekitam

WHAT DOES YOUR FAITH SPEAK ABOUT YOU?

by Mekita K. Whitfield

As a little girl growing up on the westside of Chicago, I would listen to gospel music every Sunday before heading to Sunday School with my single mother and extended family. I loved to hear the latest and greatest gospel songs playing on the local radio station 107.5 WGCI, that had the ability to stir my youthful soul. One of my favorite songs among many, was sung by a well renowned choir, The Soul Children of Chicago. The chorus of this song stated, "I might as well think big, why should anybody think small. I might as well think big if I'm going to think at all." I found myself turning up the volume on these lyrics and believing that the sky was truly the limit to what I can really have.

Residing in an extended family home with my wise grandmother, mother, two siblings, six uncles, two aunts and a few cousins. My grandfather Joseph Mathews passed away when I was only eight years of age. I recalled the times when he would come home, pick me up and toss me in the air. Oh, the joy I felt to be in the presence of my grandfather, affectionately known as "grandaddy Joe". Precious memories of grandaddy Joe lingered often and his love for me, that left an indelible impression on my heart. Our house was truly a home and at the time, it was large enough for us. There were moments when I had to pinch myself because my reality, did not appear to be real.

Growing up without the presence of my father was challenging, causing me to wonder, if I was the reason he stayed away. These moments often left me with the feeling of rejection. I found myself battling these feelings and thoughts from my childhood and spiraling into my adult life. Despite these moments, I was a dreamer and consistently found myself dreaming about my future and how I would grow up to defy the odds endured in my loving but dysfunctional family. Our roots in Christianity ran deep. My grandmother would travel the red, dirt roads in the Arkansas heat to get her children to church every Sunday. When she and my grandfather relocated to Chicago, her faith in God and ability to get her children and grandchildren to church continued.

As a child, I witnessed some life-changing moments in my adult family members lives in the home. These life-changing moments would coerce me to close my eyes and pray that it would all go away, while simultaneously believing that God would see us through. Oftentimes, I'd tell myself, when I grow up, God will enable me to go away to college and create a life different than what I witnessed. I had big plans on becoming the first college graduate in my family. It was in those moments where I began to draw closer to God and my faith in him. I began to trust God like never before. My mother taught me how to pray and why it was necessary to pray even as a child. She educated me on the power of prayer, having a relationship with God and communicating with him in my everyday life. She wanted me to know that God will always be with me, He hears me and will answer my prayers.

In the poignant words of the late Langston Hughes, "life for me aint been no crystal stair." Today I often echo the same sentiments. For life is filled with swift transitions. Life can take you places you had not intended on going. Life is filled with many ups and downs. Life can make you or break you according to your perspective and your will to fight or flee. My perspective on life consists of living in a world where you will forever experience the ebb and flow of the journey. I learned that it is not what happens to you, but merely how you react and deal with those things that you encounter daily. Life is for the living and in my opinion, one should enjoy living while benefitting from the blessings of "being on top of the dirt, and the dirt not on top of you" spoken frequently by my husband Dr. Lajuan Whitfield Sr.

Family challenges, the feelings of rejection, seeking friendships, looking to be accepted by others and my path to success was necessary in aiding to build my faith muscle. These obstacles coerced me to exercise my faith in every capacity. As a college student, I found myself writing scriptures all over my folders as a remembrance of the promises of God. I vividly recall a history class I was enrolled in where the professor declared, I was an affirmative action student and gave me an F in class based on the color of my skin. His words and that grade was enough to distract me mentally and physically from graduating in four years from the university. I reflected on Hebrews 11:1, "Now faith is the substance of things hoped for, the evidence of things not seen" (King James Version). My pastor always told me that God desired for his people to trust and obey Him. At that moment, after I cried due to the inequity, I fought against the racial injustice of the tenured professor, kept my faith intact and my testimony is, I graduated from the university in four years with my Bachelor of Arts degree and the first in my family to graduate from college.

Despite the odds that were against me, I believe by faith that I am and will always be an overcomer, in every season of my life. There have been times when I did not know how or when, but God was always on time. I'm confident in overcoming for Paul declares, "And we know that all things work together for the good to them that love God to them who are the called according to His purpose" (Romans 8:28, King James Version). I love God and I am called according to His purpose despite what it appears to be, God will get the glory out of my story. There have been times in my life when I felt like, God, where are you? However, I believed in my heart that he was there all the time and perhaps giving me an opportunity to trust Him more and exercise my faith while in the waiting room of life.

Having faith in God and exercising my faith speaks volumes. When people look at me, I am a living and walking testimony of faith in action. When people said I wouldn't make it, my faith said, yes you can. When I was denied several times, my faith said, God's delay is not denial. When I was told you don't have enough money, my faith said, God shall supply all your needs. When my business took a turn and my numbers began to plummet, my faith said, God will make the numbers count. When I made it to the age of forty people said, she's not getting married, my faith said, stand still and watch God work. To God be all glory, He set aside a man who is anointed and appointed just for me, one year happily married and a lifetime to go with my amazing husband. Regardless of what I see and hear, my belief proclaims loudly, there is no secret what faith in God can do. If it had not been for my faith in God, I would not be alive. If it had not been for my faith in God, I could not possess a healthy and positive state of mind. If it had not been for my faith in God, I would not have accomplished the goals set thus far in my life. If it had not been for my faith in God, I would not be able to share the goodness of God with you in the land of the living.

Faith talking is what I do, and faith walking is who I am. As a child of God, the bible teaches me that, "without faith it's impossible to please God" (Hebrews 11:6, King James Version). In every area of my life, I desire to please God. Do I desire to encounter trials and tribulations? No. I've learned how to exercise my faith during my trials and tribulations. Learning how to navigate the ebb and flow of life allows me to continue the daily exercise of my faith which produces, strength, peace, understanding, patience, and the knowledge of having a relationship with God, the omnipotent, omnipresent, and omniscient. There is no limit to what God can and will do in my life. As I continue to exercise my faith, I will think big, why should I think small, if I'm going to think at all, I might as well think big. So, when it is all said and done this is what my faith speaks about me!

Lord thank you for showing me what my faith speaks about me!

GLYNNIS THATCH

Glynnis Thatch is a Registered Nurse, RN, Nurse Practitioner, Functional Medicine Practitioner, Sales Director and wife to her husband of 34 years, and Mom to 3 beautiful daughters. She has worked in the medical field for 35 years and is Board Certified in Family Practice by the American Academy of Nurse Practitioners. Glynnis has been practicing as a Family Nurse Practitioner for 16 years, specializing in the Primary Care of the Family. She is the founder and CEO of Glynnis Day Thatch Consulting, LLC, where she teaches high-achieving women how to feel vibrant, attractive, and whole using a root-cause approach, so they can restore their energy, reverse health issues and reclaim their confidence.

As an Independent Sales Director, she is passionate about teaching women how to have healthy skin, look and feel great from the inside out, and empower those who want more to learn to build an entrepreneurial business of their own.

Glynnis loves spending time in devotion, mindful meditation, and exercise. Serving others is an essential part of what she does, so she believes that self-care for herself is important. Because when you take time for yourself, you can be better at serving others.

Contact Information:
glynnisthatch1@gmail.com
Facebook: /glynnis.thatch
Instagram: @glynnisthatch
(317) 919-3506

YOUR VICTORY IS IN YOUR FAITH

by Glynnis Thatch

I have always had a desire to do more. I have a strong sense of ambition. When I am surrounded by people who don't have that same pursuit for me, it makes me want to shrink. But God keeps calling me to His higher calling. It is easy to just fit in, but God didn't call me to just fit in He called me to live a life of victory and to have faith in his plans for my life.

There are external forces that have tried to keep me down. Things like me worrying about what others may say or think about me. Things like will I get the support of my loved ones. And even financially, how will I pay for the desires that I want in life? I have complete confidence and trust in God and that He is with me, for me and He is on my side. There is nothing that I have done to earn this great love that God our Father has given me. The songwriter Israel Houghton has a song that says, "who am I that you are mindful of me, that you hear me when I call?" We must have total faith that God loves us, and He hears us when we pray. We must not doubt because that will hinder our victory. How would you feel if you told your child, you would provide them with their meals, and every day they asked you, "Mom, are we going to be able to eat today?" Would you reply, haven't we been eating? And why do you doubt me? I suppose this is how God feels when we don't have total confidence and trust in his word. I personally have had a spirit of worry since I was a little kid. I would hear my dad say over and over, these words, "cast your cares upon Him for He cares for you." Or "cast your bread upon the water, and many days it shall return." He would explain to me, I know this doesn't make sense because when bread goes on water, it's going to get all soft, mushy, fall apart, so how can it return to you? The answer is we don't have to understand how, we just need to believe, in the power of God and that is where our victory lives.

I can do all things through Christ who gives me strength, Philippians 4:13. This scripture gives me faith in knowing that deep down in my soul that no matter what my flesh may be saying, nothing is impossible, and all things are possible through my faith in Christ Jesus my Lord.

I never stop holding on to the faith in God's word. Even during feeling lost, afraid, unsure, He reminds me that it does not take a lot of people supporting me because I have Him on my side. I must remember the story of Gideon. (Judges 6) when he was in battle with the Midianites. Their army was great in number, but his army was much smaller. God showed Gideon that he only needed men who were not afraid to go to war, but also who had good intentions. With only 10,000 men they defeated the Midianite army of 250,000. According to Pastor Jentezen Franklin in his book Believe That You Can, It's Time to Make it Happen, he says "there's no safer place to be than right in the center of God's will, even if that place seems to be a place of disadvantage." He calls it blessed subtraction. Where God diminishes you to develop your faith in him.

I can truly say, I have felt diminished in many areas of my life. When I say diminished, I feel as though God has brought me to a place where I am all alone. My sisters live over 500 miles from me, I don't have any close relatives nearby. God keeps reminding me over and over, that He is all I need. With him as my source I have everything I need. I can lift myself by realizing that I have been chosen by God to be in this situation at this time. The faith I have in God must translate into the faith I have in myself. Why? Because He chose me. I cannot doubt the work or will of God. He is the one who holds my life. I am victorious because He is all that I need. Consistently I am reminded of his faithfulness towards me.

Living in the victorious lane of faith has taught me to use what I have at the time. Many times, I have thought that I needed more of a certain thing to be successful. For example, more money, more education, more friends. But what I have learned is something my father, the late Elder Benjamin H. Day, used to teach us all the time. He would say "Stir what you got". God will give the increase. I recognized that my money, my education, my friends are not my source, but God is my source. He supplies all my needs according to His riches in glory.

There is a story in the book of Judges about a man named Shamgar who saved Israel. All he had was an ox-goad. An ox-goad is an instrument used to spur or guide livestock. In Judges 3:31 it talks of how this one man used his farming instrument to kill 600 Philistine men and save Israel from their enemy. Shamgar was not in the army or in a powerful position. He was a person who wanted to protect his family from the enemy. I believe that he thought if he was going to change the future of his family, he would have to do something about it, and use what he had. This is faith in action which gave them the victory.

Then, in Luke 8:43-48, there is the story of a woman who had been sick for twelve years. She came behind Jesus and touched the hem of his garment and was made whole. By her faith, she got the victory for the healing of her body.

I can see countless amounts of times where my faith in God's ability not mine, have given me the victory. Many times, the path seems impossible as if there is no way I can make it happen. However, as I continue in the path that God has called me to walk by faith in Him and not by my sight, all the while seeking God through prayer, fasting, and His Word, I will hear His voice leading me straight to the victory in Jesus and His will for my life. I am learning to lean on God like never before. I have been tempted to stay in the comfort zone of life. But I must trust that God is calling me for greater things for his Kingdom according to His will. Believe me God will ask you to do things you have never done, but remember, He is with you, and with God you cannot fail.

I said in the beginning, there will be obstacles. But see these as steppingstones to your victory. I have watched many team sports games. It's football season right now, so when I think of obstacles, I think of the defensive line. What if the offense just decided to stay in their "comfort zone" and not go for the goal of making a point? They would never have a chance of winning the game if they stayed put. But they continue to press forward for each down which moves them closer to the goal of scoring. The team believes! They have confidence, and in this context, I say they have faith that they will have the victory in scoring a point with the full intention of winning the game. So, for every tackle, these are the times when you have been knocked down, but you must be willing to get back up. These are just steppingstones to your victory. Keep the faith and continue to move forward. The bible says in Philippians 3:14, "I press towards the mark for the prize of the high calling of God in Christ Jesus." Paul the Apostle is admonishing the saints at Philippi to continue to press despite the obstacles that may come their way. He warns them earlier in the chapter to beware of evil workers, and those who will oppose them. So, this should help us understand that there will be opposition. Once we know that everything is not going to always be smooth sailing, it should give us an understanding when things don't always go our way. But we have the confidence in our God, in whom we have faith and that no matter our circumstance, He will bring us out victorious.

I encourage you to live in the faith zone. Step out of the safe zone and find your victory in your faith in God.

Thank You Lord for showing me that my Victory is in my Faith!

DR. UZOAMAKA OSILI

Dr. Uzoamaka 'Uzo' Osili is a top-producing Sales Director. In this position, she trains, inspires, and leads a team of women and men who are building their own successful businesses in the skincare and cosmetics industry.

Ms. Osili was born in Lagos, Nigeria, to an American mother and Nigerian father and lived in both countries growing up. After graduating from Princeton University, she relocated to Indianapolis, where she currently resides.

After working in the corporate sector for a few years, Ms. Osili opened and operated a wholesale/retail gift business and a temporary personnel service before being introduced to her current business. She has built and enjoyed a successful career for 32 years as an Independent Consultant and Director.

Ms. Osili is active in her church and part of the Nursing Home Ministries and the 'Academy'- teaching adult Sunday school classes. She has been a member of Alpha Kappa Alpha Sorority Inc for 40 years and is a proud recipient of an Honorary Doctorate from the TIUA School of Business. She enjoys traveling, reading, music, and spending time with family, friends, and fiancé Reed.

Contact Information:
uzomk@aol.com
(317) 471-3546

LEARNING HOW TO HAVE THE KIND OF FAITH THAT WILL MOVE THE MOUNTAINS IN YOUR LIFE

by Dr. Uzoamaka Osili

My first encounter with really exercising my faith came when I was 14. I grew up in Nigeria with an American Mother and a Nigerian (Ibo) father. My parents had met in college, married, and moved to Nigeria for my father's career.

In 1967, the Nigerian civil war had erupted. My father was visiting his hometown in the region that became Biafra. He was trapped there. Mother decided to move back to the U.S. with me and my siblings so she would have the support of her family. It was a crazy time. There were long periods where we did not know if 'Daddy' was alive or dead.
Five years passed. The war had ended, and Nigeria was rebuilding. My Mother brought me and my younger brother back to reunite with our father. My older sister was in college by then.

I thought we were there to rebuild our lives as a family. What I didn't know was that my mother had been given 2 years to live – a year earlier – and she wanted to make sure that we were reunited with our dad before she died.

The day she shared the truth with me marked the end of my childhood. Life was no longer fun and games. In addition, I wasn't allowed to tell my brother – he was too young. Plus, my dad hadn't wanted me to know yet, so I couldn't let on that I knew. It was a very lonely, painful, and frightening time.

I shared the news with my best friend because I had to talk with someone. A couple of days later she presented me with some readings on the power of faith. It was different than anything I had been taught previously. It said that I could take God's promises literally and that when I prayed, I should believe my prayers were answered and act as if it were done.

That was NOT easy. I was terrified that mother would die and leave us in this country and culture that I barely remembered with our father who we barely knew. To make things even harder, things seemed to keep getting worse. Our Mother flew back to the States to seek treatment and was told again by the 'experts' that nothing could be done. When she returned to Nigeria, she was devastated and so was I. It appeared she was getting weaker with each passing day.

At this point, my mom finally told our father that I knew. That was a small relief cause now I could cry in front of him.

After the 'death sentence' the doctors had pronounced, I began to fully immerse myself in my bible and faith readings. I began to learn and say affirmations about God's truth. I visualized Mother as healthy and happy- since according to the word, she was already healed by Jesus' stripes. This proved particularly challenging on those days when she was too weak to get out of bed.

All throughout the day, I learned to give God gratitude for the things He was doing in her life and health. There was no evidence of it in the natural. I continued to remind myself that I wouldn't need faith if I could already see the evidence.

Over the next weeks, things looked hopeless. Mother gave me her 'last instructions' talk. The things she wanted done and how to take care of my brother. Wow was that excruciating! It seemed like the end was near, but I kept affirming, visualizing, and reminding the Lord of his promises.
  My father had been experiencing severe headaches daily. He had traveled to the clinic where he got his regular checkups. As God would have it, his regular doctor was not there. The substitute doctor assured him that there was no physical reason for the problem and asked what was going on in his life. Daddy explained Mother's hopeless situation. Then the 'miracle' began.

This new doctor said he knew of 2 doctors beginning cutting edge treatments that might be able to help Mother. One doctor was in England, the other in the U.S. (Minnesota) Daddy couldn't wait to share the news. My mom was not impressed. She had been disappointed before. She only wanted to spend her remaining days with her family, not on some 'wild goose chase'. After all, she had already seen the best experts.
My dad finally convinced her to try the doctor in Minnesota. There were no guarantees, and we knew that if that team said 'no', Mother would give up trying.

I had bought a greeting card that read 'The operation's done and you're over the hump, now get well and off your rump'. It had a picture of a hippo on it. (We didn't have a large assortment of cards in Nigeria at that time.) I agonized about whether to mail it. The natural mind said, 'if you send it and they refuse her, she will be even more devastated'. My faith mind said, 'send it if you believe and she will be excited and happy that you believed'.

I mailed it. Mother received it the day after her successful surgery. She was elated. My mom who was given 2 years to live is still alive today. Hallelujah!

So, here's some of what I learned that I continue to utilize today.

1. When circumstances look bad or even horrible, find out what God's word has to say.
2. Stand on those words/promises. Repeat them in your head and out loud. Post them where you can see them many times per day.
3. Call those things that are not as though they were. Recognize that when the appearance of circumstances doesn't line up with God's word, don't allow yourself to be consumed by them (requires lots of prayer and practice)
4. Visualize the positive result that you prayed for – repeatedly.
5. Believe when you prayed that you received it.
6. Give thanks for it as done at every opportunity.
7. Practice acting and feeling as though the result is accomplished.
8. Know that God will always work things together in the best interest of His children – even when we aren't sure what that is.
9. Find someone who is a Believer and whose faith you have witnessed. Ask them for their support during the time of challenge. Some things are too heavy to bear alone.
10. Trust God and know that He loves and cares for us and that His grace is sufficient.

I am so thankful that I have learned to have the kind of faith that will move the mountains in my life!

DR. CYNTHIA MAXIE MILTON

Dr. Cynthia Milton has had a lifelong love for the arts, the art of communication, and business. Milton owns Maximum Solutions Communications, which provides marketing, public relations, and branding services for clients. She is also the CEO of Milton Properties Real Estate Investment Company.

This multiple award-winning journalist is a powerful voice in the state of Mississippi. Her rich, warm voice has endeared her to thousands of listeners, and she can be heard every morning on the radio. Milton is a news producer and local host of Morning Edition for National Public Radio affiliate WJSU at Jackson State University. She is also the host and producer of the Candid Conversations talk show, which won a first-place award from the prestigious Mississippi Association of Broadcasters. Ms. Milton has also been cited for awards by the Louisiana and Mississippi Associated Press organizations. She was also appointed as an ambassador for the City of Jackson, Mississippi, by the Metro Jackson Chamber of Commerce. In addition, Ms. Milton has lent her vocal ability and acting skills to several independent film projects and is currently recording her first single.

Contact Information:
Facebook: Cynthia Maxie Milton
Instagram: CynthiaMaxieMilton@instagram.com

STANDING FIRM IN YOUR FAITH

by Dr. Cynthia Maxie Milton

How is your faith? Has it been tested? The first two years of this new decade we survived: a worldwide pandemic. the untimely loss of loved ones and friends. wars and rumors of wars, record high inflation and gas prices, all in addition to the standard challenges of this thing we call life. It can be a test for even the most faithful believer. In times like these we must be on guard, hold on tight and stand firm on our faith. If not, the circumstances that you see, the report that you hear, can literally drain your faith tank empty.

So how do we do that? Well first we must check our foundation. We must know what faith is: how to receive faith, how to increase our faith and how to stand firm on our faith, no matter what the circumstances.

Let's start with defining exactly what faith is. The Bible says faith is the substance of things hoped for; the evidence of things not seen. In other words, faith is the building block of the thing you are believing for and your confirmation ticket even though you have not taken possession of it; yet. If you make a reservation for a room for a date one month from now, they will give you a confirmation number. That number is not a room, but it is evidence you have a room for that date at that hotel. So is our faith to us; it is evidence of the thing to come.

We can grow our faith just like we build muscles. It is important that you locate where you are in your faith. Start with believing for simple things. But don't be stagnated. Grow your faith and continue to believe for bigger things. God always wants us to grow and progress in our lives. This year your goal may be to grow your income by 10%, that is a modest goal. But the next year reach further to grow your income or business by 20%, 30% or more. As you reach milestones, exercise your faith to keep increasing them. Each achievement will help build your confidence and grow your faith.

Are you wondering how you can build your faith? By hearing, believing, and doing. The Bible says faith comes by hearing and hearing by the word of God. Many people have heard those words but too often gloss over them and treat them like a cliché. But think about what that scripture tells us. When we hear what God's word says about what we can have in His promises, faith shows up! Just by listening to faith filled words, faith arrives. It's like a summons for faith to come! This means what we allow ourselves to listen to has an impact on us and what we speak has an impact on others.

Have you ever been excited about a new project or idea? You shared it with someone. You felt certain it was a great idea, but they were negative, finding every possible reason it may not work. Could you literally feel the energy drain out of you as they spoke words of negativity over your vision or dream? Or have you ever known someone who sits around and listens to the news all day long every day, who after a while becomes a worry wart, and negative, filled with care? That's because the news tends to focus on negative things going on in our world. I am not against being informed; but if you fill up on an information diet of the news all day, your chances of becoming negative and doubtful will go up. So, it's important that we take the time to fill our minds with positive information and be around positive people. Build your faith by listening to positive messages on what you are believing for. Because, just like faith comes from hearing, so does doubt, unbelief and fear! I have a saying...Fear is faith...it's just faith for bad stuff! When you have faith for something you believe it will happen, so if you are in fear, you are in faith for bad things to happen! There is no room for fear when you are working on standing firm in your faith to reach your goals and dreams. You must guard your faith, by guarding what and who you listen to. You simply cannot share your dreams and visions with everyone.

But it is not just enough to hear and believe, we must listen and DO! The good Bible says faith without works is dead, in other words it is dead on arrival. When you have built up your faith it is time to act - to take a step to exercise your faith. It's ok to be nervous, or not have all the answers, but it's not okay to become immobilized and do nothing. You must take a step towards your goal or dream. You may say I don't know where to start. Start where you are. As you take a step towards your goal in faith, situations, people, and circumstances will begin to show up to help you. I am reminded of the story of Ms. Helen Butler, a retired schoolteacher turned real-estate investor.

She bought a property that needed to be renovated so she could rent it and begin getting a return on her investment. The day she was supposed to begin the renovation the contractor backed out. She couldn't find anyone else to do the work. She decided to just get up and go over the house and just do what she could. A short time later her big brother, Willie Milton, a savvy real-estate investor, showed up with crew in hand to help her. They got much accomplished. She took a step of faith and what she needed showed up. When you walk by faith sometimes it will look like things are not going in the direction you are trying to go. In fact, it may look like things are going in the opposite direction, but don't be swayed. A delay does not mean a denial unless you allow it to be. Keep the faith. Keep moving forward.

I heard a good friend say, "Pray and leave the details to God." It's not our job to know every detail of how something is going to work, it's our job to develop our faith and believe. I got my first speaking part in a movie after the age of forty, living in Mississippi. I don't know the statistical chances of a woman over forty getting a major speaking part in their first movie, while living in Mississippi. But I'm pretty sure they are slim.

I had an opportunity to see a screening of the movie before it was released. I enjoyed the movie but when a particular character appeared on the screen something happened to me. I got an unexplainable overwhelming longing to play the part. The director mentioned that he was looking at recasting the part. Later he held an open casting call for his production company. I auditioned for that role. He told me I had potential but went on to cast another person. At that point I could have given up. But one day while sitting on my couch and thinking about the role I said, "I don't know how but one day, someway, I will play that part!" I then got up and went to do something very mundane, like make my bed. Two hours later the director called me and offered me the part! I accepted! It was one of the most satisfying artistic experiences I've ever had. The Bible says, "Decree a thing and it shall be established." I decreed I would play the role even though all the circumstances made it look like there was no way it could happen. But I decreed it despite what things looked like. I didn't worry about how it would happen, I just believed that it would. I left the details to God, obeyed what He told me to do, and He brought it to pass! (Thank you, Jesus!)

It's our job to nurture our faith with the word and then listen to that very still small voice deep inside our spirit which will guide us in the direction we need to go. The word of God says if we acknowledge God in all ways, He will direct our path. So, get faith by listening to things that build you up and cause faith to come. And when the faith comes, pray, and believe God for your outcome, then listen to what He tells you to do and just DO It! Remember, no matter what may come, DO NOT be moved by what you see, hear or how you feel. Stand on the word. If you believe, listen, do, and won't be moved by circumstances, you will be well able to guard and stand firm in your faith. Your faith will be a force that is unstoppable!

I am so thankful to God for showing me how to stand firm in my faith.

DR. PAMELA HARVEY-COX

A native of Columbia, South Carolina, Dr. Pamela D. Harvey–Cox began her entrepreneurial journey in 2000. In January 2005, she started as the Chief Executive Officer of Pink & Proper, LLC, and in December 2021, the founder of The Pink & Proper Foundation Inc.

A graduate of Benedict College with a B.S Degree in Criminal Justice, an M.A from Webster University in Human Resources Development, and an Honorary Doctorate from TIUA School of Business. Pamela is also a Business & Entrepreneurship Certified Coach. Cox has been featured in the following publications: 2004 Times and Democrat Newspaper and 2005 The South Carolina State Newspaper Business Section. Later that year, Pam was featured in the Carolina Panorama – "A Portrait of Success" Pam Cox. Pamela has exhibited her leadership ability by inspiring, educating, and coaching others on how to be successful entrepreneurs. One of her best-known gifts is the ability to teach people skills needed to attain personal and professional success. Cox is passionate about making a difference for others and believes what you give to the life of others returns to yours.

Pamela D. Harvey-Cox currently resides in Columbia, South Carolina.

Contact Information:
(803) 397-6044
pinkandproper@gmail.com
Facebook: facebook.com/pinkandproper

LEARNING HOW TO BELIEVE WITH YOUR HEART AND CONFESS WITH YOUR MOUTH YOUR FAITH

by Dr. Pamela Harvey-Cox

July 1983 was the year that changed my heart. You see my family matriarch left this earth. Now, we all know that wisdom comes in many forms, and it was my grandmother who poured those nuggets and continued to speak to me even in her eternal life, which shaped my belief in knowing that having "faith" the size of a mustard seed is worth more than gold. More importantly, I realized the power of believing in my heart that all things are possible and mastering the art of manifestation has served me well throughout my 55 years of living my life to its fullest. (Romans 10:9–10 NKJV) That if you confess with your mouth the Lord Jesus and believe in your heart that God has raised Him from the dead, you will be saved. (10) For with the heart one believes unto righteousness, and with the mouth, confession is made unto salvation.

As I reflect, there is true power in the tongue. Intently being aware of every word that I speak and ensuring that each word aligns with my heart and the desires of my heart be loud and clear! Let me go back to my grandmother. I would like to think that in my younger years I was a "good" granddaughter being obedient at every chance that presented itself. Unfortunately, I fell short as we all do as children.

The "Prayer & The Quilt"! "Now, I lay me down to sleep I pray to the lord my soul to keep if I should die before I wake, I pray to Lord my soul to take." That prayer alone started me on my journey to meditate on every word I confess out of my mouth. Here comes the "Quilt" after the prayer like clockwork and in my mind it symbolized security. Grandma tucked me in and that is in my mind a "safe" place. That quilt felt like the heaviest covering anyone one could have over them in a physical sense. However, there is a covering over all our lives that keeps us safe. I am eternally grateful. Then her comforting words no matter how our day went sounded like this, "Pamela, you are going to do great things just believe in your heart and take no other thought." Grandmother knew exactly what seeds she was planting. So grateful for her in all her wisdom. She spoke belief and I started to learn how to believe.

It was my first year in college that these words would come to me again it was her speaking to my spirit and yes if we pay attention our spirit is being fed every moment of our incredible lives if we are open and aware that the universe gives us exactly what we are expecting. Finding my way through this journey called life there has been one thing that has remained constant, my ability to believe wholeheartedly that I (we) can have what we say we can have.

It seemed as if I was all alone and here, she comes. The joy of knowing that her spirit was with me then and still to this very day was all that I needed, with the faith and belief that what I believed in would happen. Believing in my heart means believing apart from your mind and body. Thinking is of the mind; believing is of the heart. When knowing the difference, made a difference. In every instance, the heart must be free of any past guilt, disappointments, and failures. Here is the reality of it all: first, things are not always what they seem as you hold the power to see it only as you want it to manifest. Secondly, committing to face challenges head-on and creative avoidance can be detrimental to your growth. Knowing that I must face certain challenges but choosing the ones that I felt would be easy may not have been the ones to change the outcome for what I believed in my heart. Finally, eradicate all liabilities and keep faith first. It all comes together masterfully. In moments of chaos, all things are working in your favor.

Growing up in a single-parent household and seeing what determination looks like from the daughter of my grandmother was yet another thing that helped shape my thought process. Yes! My mother, the offspring of my angel of a grandmother made it her goal to feed only good things into my soul while taking on the major task of parenting alone. One of the earliest examples of believing in your heart and having enough faith to see it manifest was to have lived in what some may call the projects or low-income housing and your mom telling you, "We may live here now but I will become the manager of this housing complex" and she did just that. Consequently, the position increased her income which allowed her to buy our first family home as a single parent. It would be many years later that history would repeat itself in my personal life.

So many twists and turns make you wonder what route is the one that will lead you to your desired destination. Guess what, we never know but big belief and faith will have us continue to confess and declare what happens at the end of the road. Amazingly, what we expected to be at the destination is exactly what shows up!

The heart is the gateway, what's inside will undoubtedly come out. Learning how to believe was a simple choice for me because any other options would leave me empty on the inside. I needed to understand that speaking based on my faith would serve me in all aspects of my life. Become relentless in your belief and be all-knowing that once you have prayed and asked God, "no matter what life brings" your heart will always smile. Surrender and know that your faith will see you through all things and you must not waver in believing that it is already done. No begging is needed. Once you have prayed, take comfort in knowing you have been heard.

Lord thank you for showing me how to believe with my heart and confess with my mouth my faith.

DR. LONDON SPIVEY

I have been in the wellness industry since 2000. I am passionate about teaching nutrition and what it truly takes to live a balanced and healthy life. Whether I'm training for a fitness competition, a marathon, or just maintaining enough energy to keep up with my kids, I've learned that nutrition is the foundation of a healthy lifestyle.

While attending the University of Houston, I explored many paths. I was a theater actress and a runway model, and I was employed at a fitness center. I discovered my passion there, and in 2006 I opened my fitness studio, Inspired Fitness. In 2011, I penned my first book/nutrition guide, *Fit In 40 Days: A Nutrition Daily Devotional*. The following year I closed my studio and began a career in the financial industry. In June of 2022, I was bestowed an Honorary Doctorate Degree from Trinity International University of Ambassadors (TIUA). Today, I am an entrepreneur wearing many hats, including wellness coaching for Fit In 40 Days.

Using social media platforms, I teach the importance of healthy eating and provide the information needed to be successful with the Fit In 40 days program.

Contact Information:
www.londonspivey.com
Admin@londonspivey.com
IG: @londonspiveyofficial
FB: /londonsj

LEARNING HOW TO HAVE FAITH DURING YOUR STORM

by Dr. London Spivey

Hebrews 11:1 says, "faith is the substance of things hoped for and the evidence of things not seen." Webster's Dictionary defines faith as, "a firm belief in something for which there is no proof."

Faith can also be the belief that an event or circumstance will occur in the future. Since none of us can predict the future, nearly everything we do is an act of faith. Because tomorrow isn't promised, simply making plans is an act of faith. Creating a schedule is an act of faith. Getting in your car. Going to work. Sending your kids to school. Nearly everything can be considered an act of faith. We all practice faith to some extent because faith is easy when things are going according to plan. It's easy to have faith when you have a steady job, food in the refrigerator and money in the bank. It's easy to have faith when the plan is working, and you are working the plan.

What about those times when the plan isn't working? When the job you prayed for is more demanding than you thought it would be. What if the people you work with act like devils and make your life difficult? What happens when "love, honor and cherish" turn into disdain, resentment, and neglect? When everything you believed to be true is completely the opposite. Will you have faith then?

In 2009, I cried out to God for answers and guidance. I begged for His help and the response I heard was, "You don't want my help. "What does that mean?

Of course, I wanted God's help. Not only did I want help- but I also needed answers. I needed to know why this was happening to me. ME! I had done everything right. I made excellent grades in school, and I was the President of my class. I played sports, graduated college, then got married and had two beautiful children. I did everything right and I did them in order. So why was I here? How did I end up so lost, confused, and unsure of my decisions? Nothing in my life was living up to my expectations. Not even the expectations I had of myself. I needed answers and I needed help. I was depressed, desperate, and God's response was...

"You don't want my help." Romans 10:13 says, "Whoever calls on the name of the Lord shall be saved." So, why wasn't God saving me? Why wasn't God helping me? I have been in the church my entire life. My mom dragged me to every church meeting, prayer meeting, cry meeting, woman's meeting... I went everywhere with my mom. And I heard EVERYTHING! As the youngest of five kids, I was my dad's 'baby girl' and I was the cute, innocent baby sister. We had a big family and there was no shortage of drama. I watched my siblings go through life's trials like a fly on the wall. Taking it all in, learning from their mistakes, taking notes, and creating a plan of action. I knew exactly what I was going to do or not do. I knew exactly what I was going to put up with. I knew it all. I had it all figured out.

I had it ALL figured out. "I" had it all figured out... I... I... I .... thus, the reason God said, "You don't want my help."

I wanted God's help, but I wasn't ready to receive the help. I wasn't ready to let go and fully trust Him. I wasn't ready to go where He told me to go. Leave when He told me to leave. Release when He told me to release. Hang on when He told me to hang on. I wasn't ready to take one step before knowing the destination.

Sure, I had faith. I had faith that everything would work out because it always does. God has always provided for my needs and taken care of me. Even when I didn't feel like I deserved it. But did I have enough faith to follow God down a path that looked grim and hopeless? Did I have enough faith to make a move that would break my heart, but give me peace? Did I have enough faith to let go of my pride? Did I have enough faith to do things I said I would never do? Did I have enough faith to let it all fall apart? God was right. I didn't want His answers. I didn't want His help. I wasn't ready.

So, God let me continue walking on the path I had chosen. He allowed me to struggle, fall, cry, give up, try again, and go around in circles until I found myself in the same spot ten years later. In 2019 I cried out to God again, but this time I was tired. Despite my best efforts, my plan wasn't working. My life looked great on the outside, but the inside was a mess. I had the good, safe job that my husband wanted me to have. I've always been an entrepreneur and I've never had the desire to pursue a '9 to 5'. This job made him happy, not me. We had two kids, a dog, a house, but my husband and I rarely spent time together. We hardly ever slept in the same room. We never went on dates. The part that hurt most was that he didn't seem to mind. We tried counseling a few times over the years and my requests for more counseling was met with a hard, unbudging

"No". We took vacations, but they were just another part of the show. An act. At this point I refused to waste more money on useless vacations where all we did was fight and argue the whole time. Why fly to Mexico to fight when we can argue at home? I was dying inside and I'm sure he was too. Although, when asked, he claimed he was happy. I found that hard to believe.

After watching a counseling show on television, I realized that I had to do something about my marriage. I had to do something about my life. I didn't want to repeat family cycles and leave it to my children to break the cycles. I did not want my children to find themselves in this same position one day. I accepted that this was too much for me to fix. After all, I was the one who got myself into this mess. I cried out to God again and this time I surrendered. "Lord, just tell me what to do and I'll do it." "... for truly I say to you, if you have faith the size of a mustard seed, you will say to this mountain, 'Move from here to there,' and it will move; and nothing will be impossible to you." -Matthew 17:20 I didn't know where God was going to lead me, but I was willing to take the chance. I didn't know the plan, but it didn't matter. I'd survived every storm to this point, and I had complete faith that God would carry me through any other storm that crossed my path. That year God gave me answers.

The answers were difficult to accept, and I struggled with them. I questioned God and I cried for months. God are You sure this is what I should do? Am I hearing You correctly Lord? Why must it happen this way? He opened my eyes to so many things. I had to make some tough decisions, face some hard truths and I had to let it all fall apart. Letting it all fall apart was the best thing I did for myself. Letting God be God, was the best thing I did for myself and my family.
To this very day the storms continue to come but living a life of faith is so rewarding. Living a life of faith requires courage. Living a life of faith requires tenacity. Living a life of faith requires determination.

I've learned to stay out of God's way and just let God be God. When He gives me a vision, a desire, or an idea, I simply thank Him for it and carry on with my day. I don't concern myself with the "how". I don't worry about "how" something will happen or "how" things will come together. I let God be God. Period. And He shows up every time.

I have learned how to have faith during the storms of life!

SONJI NEVERSON

Sonji Neverson, born and raised in Boston, Massachusetts, is highly motivated and inspired by Gospel, fashion, beauty, and music. Currently, an Independent Beauty Consultant, working in direct sales of skin care products and promoting self-image and mentoring skills for women.

Married to Maurice Neverson Jr. II, they share three boys and two girls. Sonji, who was raised Muslim, is now a born-again Christian since1998. Her church home is Eagle Heights Cathedral in Revere, Massachusetts, where Bishop Dr. James E. Collins is the Pastor. Sonji served as a member of the choir and Worship Team for 16 years and has been an active member for 22 years. Prior to becoming a Christian, Sonji pursued an intense career in Pop and R&B during the 80s, working with Grammy-nominated music producers. Sonji's band performed opening acts for internationally known Pop groups.

Presently she and her husband minister together as "Mauson Majesty," called to minister through Inspirational and Gospel music. They have recorded original music that can be found on YouTube. Their most recent single is called "America." "I'm looking forward to making a difference in my life and others through my business and being instrumental in advancing the Kingdom of God through music."

Contact Information:
(781) 656-3575
Sonji.teamjoy@gmail.com
FB: Sonji Neverson
Instagram: Sonji Neverson
YouTube: Maurice & Sonji Neverson

BEING RELENTLESS ABOUT YOUR FAITH

by Sonji Neverson

I remember as a child growing up Muslim, my parents would take me to the Mosque where I participated in all religious activities and events. I would look forward to praying and fasting during Ramadan as my second-grade teacher would reward the students with ice cream. I remember my siblings trying to force me to eat during the time of Ramadan. I refused to let up. I was very dedicated with attending the mosque because I had a love for God.

As a Muslim child I was told that Christianity was not the black man's true religion. That troubled me!! I struggled with this because I had so much love for people, no matter the color of their skin. Born in the 60s I dreamed that people of all nations would be together.

My heart was broken when my parents left the Mosque leaving me and my siblings in despair without a practicing faith. I asked my mother at the time "what do we do now?" I remember my mom saying to me "always love God and to pray at home". My mom enrolled us in public school. We still called ourselves Muslims, continued to pray to Allah as God and I fasted during Ramadan.

I grew up in a musical family with 9 siblings and my brother was instrumental in supporting my ability to sing. I began an intense career singing Pop and R & B music. I was determined to get a recording contract, so I dedicated my time to recording late nights in the studio as I continued to work full-time. During this season my life drastically changed because of unforeseen circumstances that forced me and my sisters to leave home without warning. I was offered opportunities in the broadcasting industry but felt I was too shy, yet I was determined to accomplish my dreams. Working very hard in the music industry, I wanted a normal life, like being married and having a family. I saw myself heading down a slippery slope. The lessons of holiness, fearing God and obeying His commandments came to memory. I felt there was hope and I dreamed of a better life.

I believed my life was about to change when I met a woman who invited me to this business event which I believed was an answer to my prayer. I'll never forget walking in the room and seeing an array of positive women from multi-cultures. Displaying high self-esteem as their confidence lifted the room, I joined them that night. I connected and I saw myself being one of them. I placed my career of becoming a pop artist on hold to pursue this newfound opportunity. This was also an opportunity to sharpen my personal skills which I felt I needed.

I was learning to set goals and hold presentations. My confidence was progressing. I began singing at business events and realized I could utilize all by gifts in a positive way. As a Muslim, even though I was invited to Church on numerous occasions, I was not planning to attend a Christian service. Little did I know I was asked to do makeup and sing at Church services for weddings and I'm hearing the Holy Biblical Word of God for the first time.

Just when I thought I was making headway to turn my life around, life happened. I was winning in my business when I unexpectedly became a single mom. I had been trapped in relationships I never anticipated. I finally came to a place and realized I needed to do things God's way for myself and my son. My relentless search for God began.

There were several women that God used to be instrumental in my path to Christ. One was Nora Shariff-Borden a Muslim. She taught my first class, and I had the privilege of spending time at her home. I watched her climb the ladder of success and witnessed her setbacks. I then took time away to care for my newborn son. When I returned, this amazing woman I knew as a Muslim was now preaching the gospel of Jesus Christ.

Stunned, I asked, "How did you become a Christian". I was at a place of brokenness, and she was full of Joy. I wanted that in my life but believed it wasn't possible. I was a Muslim. With words of wisdom this woman instructed me to pray. A circle was formed, and others began to pray for me. The Word spoken to me was that God heard my prayer. It was 14 years after leaving home and 7 years of searching. I began to pray to Allah and Jesus. I became desperate to know God. I asked God to show me a sign and he did. I was invited to Christian events witnessed healing, deliverances, and other miracles.

The most exciting day of my life has come. October 11, 1998. Columbus Day weekend. The search was on. During this season of prayer my director announces an exciting new retreat for consultants is coming designed for education, inspiration, and motivation. It was not mandatory, but we were given an opportunity to attend the Sunday Devotion. I didn't understand Devotion was like being at a Church service. I was excited to attend the training. The Word preached that morning was "I surrender all". I knew God was calling for me. The song was playing as I made my way to the altar. I took a step by faith that day even though I did not know who Jesus was. I recited the sinner's prayer. I didn't understand the virgin birth or how Jesus was God's Son because I had witnessed supernatural miracles. I wanted to know more.

At the altar, I remember hearing the cheers from my peers who were praying for me. I was given a bracelet that read "what would Jesus do?" I received it as my first assignment. I was given Word that I would find a Church home and a Pastor that would give me direction. He will be like my dad. Currently, I was being reminded of the pain of my dad not being present in my life for 15 years now. I was ordered to stay at this Church even when I didn't understand and to always place my trust in God. When you find this Church, you will know that its God.

I want to thank my friend Flow Simmons an African woman of God who was instrumental in my walk with Christ. Just as I was instructed, I visited Churches but didn't connect. I became distracted by a relationship and began to grow weary. But God had a way of allowing things to happen that forced me right back on track. I was dealing with a lot more than I could handle on my own. I called my friend Flow and asked if she knew of a place that I could go to pray. I was being forced to find a private school for my son. Flow said, I heard about a Church that is near your home. The following Sunday was Easter Sunday. I thought, perfect.

I walked in and first saw all the classrooms. Making our way into the sanctuary, the first thing I saw, the Pastor was singing like my dad. Both he and his wife resembled my parents the way they looked when I was a child. Their daughters resembled my sisters.

The multi-cultural children's choir came rushing through singing and dancing carrying flags of every nation. I felt I was dreaming. It was my first experience of a multi-cultural Church. It resembled the business meetings I attended. I remember crying the entire service and making my way to the altar a second time. This time I received my first Bible and met my Bishop.

I want to conclude first giving thanks to my Lord and Savior Jesus Christ. When unwillingly led astray, He brought me back to where I belonged. I learned to trust God through every door that opened and every door that closed by prayer and by reading His Word. Currently I've been a member of my Church for 22 years and saved for 24. I was baptized there, met my husband and we raised 2 handsome sons there. Early on I joined the Church choir and sang on the worship team for 16 years while recording gospel music with my husband.

I'm grateful for the Holy Spirit who has been guiding me all along. What seems like a long journey feels like a new beginning. Below are a few of my favorite scriptures that helped me to understand what it means to be relentless about your faith or anything that God calls you to or a battle in your life that you may be facing.

My moto is Never Give Up. When the going gets tough. Stay in the race; Keep going!! And pray, pray, pray.

1. Hebrews 11:6 "It is impossible to please God without faith." While I was praying to Allah and Jesus this scripture came to me while reading a book.
2. Isaiah 55:8-9. "For your thoughts are not your thoughts neither are your ways declares the Lord"
3. Proverbs 3:5-6 "Trust in the Lord with all your heart and lean not on your own understanding. In all your ways acknowledge Him; submit to Him and He will direct your path.
4. Ephesians 2:8-9: "For by grace you have been saved through faith and this is not your own doing; it is the gift of God, not a result of works, so that no one may boast."

I am so thankful that God has shown the importance of being relentless about my Faith!

ARDRA SINETT

Ardra Sinett, Saint Louis, MO native, University of Kansas graduate, the "Show-Me" Peach, is a Foodpreneur: Certified Herbalist, Certified Nutritionist, Certified "Drop-theMic" Speaker, Certified Essential Colors Facilitator, Certified Match Maker, Etiquette Coach, Ordained Minister, Artist, Actress, Model, Host, Brand Ambassador, Chef, Baker & CEO.

She has been on an Entrepreneurial journey since 1993 when she became a Beauty Consultant for the first time. She has been twirling around the Atlanta food scene since 2008, making a historic impression in the community and on the social scene. Making cakes for everyone from Mary J. Blige to Barrack Obama; 100's of magazine spreads Nationally in Essence and locally recognized in many papers, blogs, podcasts, and on magazine covers. Ardra has appeared in 250+ movies, tv shows, commercials, PSA's, and food competition shows.

Her commitment to community is always her most critical mission. She is the recipient of the Presidential Life-Time Achievement Award and the Delta Sigma Theta Award for Community Excellence. Her 501c3 Non-Profit: Taste Love CDC has been supplying birthday parties for kids 1-18 whose parents are incarcerated, in shelters, or deceased since 2008.

Her website and YouTube channel: Cooking Couture Atlanta, are home to her Entertaining Daily Content and food centered merchandise, from custom charcuterie serving boards to a food game that accesses your personality based on what you eat. This CEO Chef is a complete meal that has to be experienced not just eaten.

Contact Information:
(770) 742-8549
www.cookingcoutureatlanta.com
IG/Twitter: @cookingcoutureatl
Youtube: CookingCoutureAtlanta
www.YouTube.com/cookingcoutureatlanta
Facebook: CookingCoutureAtlanta
Ardra@cookingcoutureatlanta.com

WALKING BY FAITH WHEN THERE IS NO EVIDENCE

by Ardra Sinett

FAITH ONLY EXISTS IN THE DARK WHEN YOU ARE TOTALLY BLIND TO THE OUTCOME IF YOU CAN SEE IT... IT DOESN'T REQUIRE FAITH.

It was 04-15-2015 around 10 am est. all my business locations were invaded, seized, and closed by a task force led by the State of Georgia Dept of Revenue and accompanied by the IRS, ATF, GBI all being filmed by the local ABC Affiliate WSB-Atlanta. I was initially watching all this go down on my cell phone, shocked with my mouth literally wide open, through my security cameras until they discovered and disconnected them. They entered with Driver's License Pictures of everyone that they wanted to speak with, mainly me and my management team. After an hour they let most of the staff go, after about 5 hours they released my management team. They were trying to really get me to come back to the location so that they could truly humiliate me on camera, live TV with agents everywhere, customers and clients watching. I knew better than that or my dismayed anxiety caused a "self-protecting" apprehension that prevented me from even considering returning to that alleged scene of the crime.

They kept calling me and having my employees call me, saying they just wanted to talk. I was paralyzed and afraid and I felt very alone.

When I got up off the ground, knees wet from my tears, I'd cried so much my tears weren't even salty anymore, my face was numb, fingernails missing, and my tracks were sliding from me pulling my hair. I literally wanted to cause myself so much physical pain that it would distract me from the devastating avalanche of mental and emotional anguish that was lying before me totally blocking my future and any growth and any symbolism of resilience.

Before that day, I loved to brag that my strongest traits were my bulldog tenacity and resilience, but never ever before had I lost EVERYTHING, and it was televised! I thought I was going to self-combust and die! It felt like all the humiliation, the disappointment and the scary, searing, looming sadness was turning into hot volcano lava inside of me that would surely burn up all my internal organs and I would just lay down on the floor and be no more. I laid on the floor waiting to be put out of my misery. Honestly, with the sincerest vulnerability right now, I confess I did not want to be here among more. I simply couldn't imagine how I could possibly prosper through this moment in time. It was so heavy, that I was so seriously stuck!

I've never just wanted to live life. I have always wanted to win, to be first, to be impressive! If I couldn't have it all I didn't want anything. At that moment I was completely blind to any possibility of a triumph.

I was continually being reminded of the time passing – time that I would never get back. If I wasn't going to die, I had to make a move, I couldn't just sit in sadness and self-pity. However, I don't think my brainwashing or brainwashers could have been aware of exactly what catastrophes the future had been holding for me. Nonetheless, the only thing I knew to do at that time was to rely on what had been sown and planted inside me. All the tapes I had listened to, the cd's, books, conferences, trainings, workshops, and the word of God. It was time to put all that stored up power into action and it began with activating my faith. Faith would prove to be my superpower and after 24 hours (way over my limit) no matter how bad I felt I was committed to have faith and leaned into it. I decided to get up off my knees, I metaphorically fell on my back and looking up to the sky the only word I received, the only concept that pierced my spirit was... Now faith is the substance of things hoped for, the evidence of things not seen! Hebrews 11:1. I was certainly going to have to find a way over, under or through this trauma and in my darkest, saddest, sleepless moments I knew through faith, it was all working together for my good.

I was hearing a constant soft calming whisper in my ear: If you would just have faith as that of a mustard seed... (Luke 17:6) everything will be alright.

It was time to put it all to the test. I had no choice but to let my journey of walking in this concept of faith begin. I had professed all my adult life that I had faith, that I was a "believer" I now had no choice but to believe and then to activate my Faith.

I had no choice but to lean into my Faith. I accepted and realized that I was the narrator of my future. I had to regain control of this story which was mine and mine alone to direct. With very little strength and no energy, I couldn't see what the future possibly had in store for me, so I felt I had no choice but to blindly walk in this thing called faith. Now no matter what it looked like with my eyes and no matter what was going on around me in the physical, even if it was on TV all weekend on repeat and my so-called friends were posting the news story on theirs and my Facebook pages, it was time to believe and speak life into myself, a power that I believed was granted to me at Calvary. I had to pretend, and force myself to believe, stand and walk as if everything that was going on was working together for my GOOD! It was nothing that anyone else could do for me. Activating your Faith is a personal, individual relationship thing with your God.

The intensity of your faith is the truest reflection of your relationship with your higher power. You can say what you want, but your FAITH shows and proves it all. I got a lawyer and I think I got the worst lawyer in all Dekalb County GA. I set a meeting with the devils and walked into the Lion's Den with nothing but my Faith to protect and guide me. They talked in circles until the news cameras were in place outside unbeknownst to me, and then the nicely dressed gentleman with the bow tie and the one dressed in jeans and a t-shirt arrested me and took me outside for my 'walk of shame' in front of the live cameras, but no employees, no customers or passersby. I was able to bond myself out of jail for just $12 (admin fee). I was the first person in Georgia to ever be charged with the charge I received. The $12 was for the issuing of the new docket numbers. They just created a charge for me that day, how special!

When I was sitting in the holding cell the TV commercial for my business aired, what serendipity. The ladies in the cell looked at me, took a double take, and asked, "are you the CAKE LADY?" I just stared straight ahead with tears in my eyes and a strange feeling of relief falling all over me. I didn't have the strength to move my lips, but on the inside, I was saying not anymore.

In less than 6 months after the expedited auction and intense ignominy I received a letter from the State stating that there would be no charges and all allegations and inquiries were being dropped and I could go back to business as usual.

This is where one might think the celebration and exhilaration would begin, where I would fall to my knees in gratitude to God. One might think that this alone proved the validity and power of this thing called faith. Well, that's not what happened at all. I was happy the charges were dropped, but I was hurt, I was angry and most intensely I was disappointed in myself. How could I have let this happen, with all my knowledge, insight, and faith, how did this all happen to me.

It was surprisingly the beginning. Had I known there would be more:

lessons to learn, spiritual muscles to develop, insight to receive, I might have laid on that floor a little longer.

First you must believe, and belief alone can take you a very long way, but for anything else substantial and powerful to happen, your Faith must be activated. This was the beginning of me defining what FAITH would come to mean to me and my life:
F A I T H = Forgiving ARDRA Intentionally, Trusting & Healing.

When you activate your faith, you define your relationship with God and your higher self. Faith is the key that unlocks everything the heavens have for you; it's how you discover your purpose and live in your passion. Faith led me on a journey of intentionality that will forever be my calling card and the one sure legacy I will leave this world; this journey forever changed the trajectory of my life.

Was it the actions of 04-15/16-2015? Was it surviving being face to face with a nervous breakdown? Was it the powerful love and support I received from only a very select few of people that made this exercise in Faith so astounding?

What was indeed life-changing and powerful was realizing that my entire life to that point had been my faith walk. Romans 10:17 says "Faith cometh by hearing, and hearing by the word of God". So, all the lectures, speeches, tapes, conferences, workshops, sermons, revivals... I was hearing and I was building and storing. At any time, I could have activated my blind faith and walked in its fullness, but I had opted like many to settle for storing it, building it up to activate later. It would then come to a point in my existence that there was no other choice for me. You will come to a space in time where you will have to make a choice to blindly trust and walk in what you know, what you have stored up inside you. It will be the only way you will win, or you will cop out and not experience the fullness that is there for you. The power to overcome the trauma that was facing me had to be unlocked and activated through truly blindly walking in this very real unseen thing called Faith. Once activated, the realization and acknowledgement of it opened me up to a realm of existence that is so powerful and life-changing and ever evolving, it's something you won't see coming. Because, if you can see it, it really isn't true faith. If I had to give you any advice it would be to learn how to walk by faith and not by sight as I did on 04-15-2015.

I am so thankful to God that I was able to walk by Faith when there was no evidence!

DR. LISA YVETTE JONES

Lisa Yvette Jones, the Chief Caring Officer of iC.A.R.E. Leadership, LLC. Lisa supports professional women leaders to maximize their leadership influence, to C.A.R.E. (Cultivate Authentic Relationships to Empower), and to live out their Self-Care S.U.C.C.E.S.S. while holistically transforming and humanizing the employment experience, head, hands, and heart.

Although Lisa has over 30 years in the Federal Sector, as a leader, she is passionate about coaching, training, and leading successful, high-performance, and well-balanced teams. She is also a highly sought-out mentor and leadership trainer for her agency.

Having conquered a deadly cancer health crisis and releasing over two hundred pounds, Lisa knows that self-care for leaders is necessary. As an early-detection cancer evangelist for the American Cancer Society, Lisa also saves lives by promoting cancer awareness.

Lisa is a John Maxwell Certified Leadership Coach, Teacher, Trainer, Speaker, Les Brown Power Voice Systems Graduate, and an International Amazon Best-Selling Author.

Contact Information:
Facebook: /lisa.yvette.jones
Instagram: @lisayvettejones2
Twitter: lisayvettejone1
Youtube: youtube.com/channel/UCRfcWjiueMYk7nxxXQWPZYQ
Club House: @thecaringleaderer

LEARNING HOW TO CHOOSE
THE ROAD OF FAITH

by Dr. Lisa Jones

There is not a day that goes by when we are not considering our choices, i.e., what to wear, what to eat, who to talk to, what to purchase, to pray or not to pray? Choices are a part of the human experience. It is the one distinctive element of our existence that separates us from all of God's creation. We, as human beings, have the divine inherited right to choose. Whether good or evil, right, or wrong, we make choices that not only affects the trajectory of our lives, but also the lives of others. Some of our choices are great and we have no regrets; however, let us face it, there are many of our other choices that have been the catalyst of our grief, sorrow, and disappointments.

I am most grateful to our creator, God, as I know and believe, He chose me and my purpose, well before the foundations of this world. In fact, I have chosen to coin myself as God's Ephesian's 2:10 Woman: "For we are [I AM] his workmanship, created in Christ Jesus for good works, which God prepared ahead of time for us [me] to do." (Eph. 2:10, CSB). The book of Jeremiah goes on the say, "For I know the thoughts that I think toward you, saith the Lord, thoughts of peace, and not of evil, to give you an expected end." (Jer. 29:11, KJV). I choose to believe that there is greatness in me to live out those thoughts and plans and to live a life of vitality while doing so.

April of 2009, my birthday month, I decided to give myself a gift. You know ladies, that gift that we give ourselves every year, that yearly appointment that we dread, but it is also, the appointment that we know that we must keep. That appointment turned into another appointment and before I knew it, I was before two gynecologic oncologists. With empathy and concern, I heard these words, "Ms. Jones, you have been diagnosed with stage three Cervical Cancer -Papillary Serous Carcinoma of the cervix. It is high grade, and it is quite vicious, so much so, that it is eating through your body."

I then had a shock wave go through my body. I could not understand how such destruction was raging so viciously inside of me and that could potentially kill me. My intelligent brain could not comprehend this news because I had not one symptom or irregularity and there was no history of cancer in my family. There was no precursor for this diagnosis, but was there a precursor? At the time of my diagnosis, I was every bit of 362 pounds. I looked good and I felt good. If I did not think it and believe it, then nobody else would, right? Well, because I needed more information and a better understanding, I did what any intelligent person would do, I began my research. Studies would reveal that those 362 pounds were my warning, my precursor for cancer and for my life.

Studies conducted by the Centers for Disease Control (CDC) reflect that 40% of the cancers in America are related to obesity. Wow! Now please know, I am not saying that everyone who is obese will have cancer, what I am saying is that the science does reflect that there is a cancer/obesity link. In fact, there are thirteen cancers in the United States that have been linked to obesity. A few of them are breast cancer, thyroid cancer, ovarian cancer, liver cancer-to name a few.

I advised the doctors that I needed some time. The doctors reminded me that because of the viciousness of the cancer that they diagnosed me with, I did not have time. Notice my language, the cancer that they diagnosed me with. I never took ownership of that diagnosis by staking claim to it by saying, "I have cancer." No! I refused too! It was not that I did not believe that the diagnosis was not true, I was not going to give it life, through my choice of words. My good book says, "Death and Life are in the power of the tongue...!" I then knew that since I was in a fight for my life; I had to choose the words of life and faith.

The doctors advised that if I did not have the surgery within the next few days, but no later than a week, I would certainly die because once the cancer spread to any major organ, they would not open me up. Both doctors gave me two death sentences. I continued to believe that healing was my destiny, and my faith was the road to my total recovery. I also could not fathom a premature death for me. Therefore, I insisted that I needed time to retreat, fast, pray, and hold on to my faith that God is who He said He is – my Healer!

After leaving the doctor's office and while seated in my car with this dark storm cloud over my life, I called on a few key people who knew the words and the worth of prayer, including my now late ex-husband. He was so kind and compassionate. He unselfishly stood with me and by me during my entire ordeal. Besides, we both share an amazing son, Anthony Maurice Jones, II, who was only 14 years young at the time of this news about his momma. It is imperative that you know those who will choose to stand in faith with you when you are facing a storm, and in my case as with many of you, death.

It was time to put my faith to the test for me. As a minister, I have counseled with, prayer for, and have ministered to many others regarding choosing the power of their faith during their turmoil. It was now time for me to take the years of what I poured into others, to now look in the mirror of my faith and believe it for me. I did. I shut out all to shut into God. On the third day of my fasting and praying, the storm had subsided, and I heard these words, "It is not unto death. You shall live and not die, and this will never return!" I knew it! Because Gods plans and purpose for me were not over. The waves of concern were boisterous, but the fight for my life was greater than the waves attempting to overtake me.

I then gave thanks and praise to my sustainer of life, my Chief Physician - God. I then made the appointment to return to the oncologist. I informed the doctor of what I had heard from my Chief Physician. The doctor then understood Who I was speaking about. I further advised the doctor that although their diagnosis is serious and quite troubling; however, my Chief Physician's prognosis is what I will live by. I advised the doctor that I would have surgery on June 29, 2009, and I further reminded the doctor that there was no further spreading of the deadly disease. The doctor was not convinced and then told me again that I would die if I waited that long, over one month from my original diagnosis. The disease was too deadly. I then assured the doctor of my faith in God.

The doctor reluctantly said, "Why do I have a feeling that I will see you on June 29th?" I said, "Because you will." And he did! I had the surgery to remove the cancer and it was undoubtedly a success - a faith and prayer success!

I have since released over two hundred pounds and counting! My faith made me whole! Our lives are a gift from God and what we do with our life by living out our purpose is our gift to the world that awaits us.

Below are a few of several bonus strategies that were the catalyst to my successful journey of courageously navigating the Cancer Storm of Life by choosing to put my faith and trust in God's hands:

1. P.R.A.Y.
   a. **P**raise God
   b. **R**eflect on all He has already done for you.
   c. **A**dorn Him, His Goodness, His Grace, and His Mercy
   d. **Y**ield fully to His presence and His purpose for your life.

2. Trust God with all your heart. (Proverbs 3: 5-6)

3. Since you are a partner in your health care; be relentless about advocating for your own health.

4. Never take your health for granted; therefore, schedule and keep all

appointments. Remember, I had no symptoms and was already in Stage 3 of a very vicious cancer diagnosis.

5. Know your numbers and record the date:
       a. How much do you weight? _____/_____
       b. What is your blood pressure? _____/_____
       c. Cholesterol level? _____/_____
       d. A1C/blood sugar level? _____/_____
       e. Blood type? _____/_____

The doctors may have given me that diagnosis of Stage 3 Cervical Cancer, and two death sentences, but my Chief Physician gave the prognosis of life! Each June 29th, I celebrate another year of victorious navigation of a vicious storm of life. I am still here! The storm may have been a formidable force to manage, but choosing the road to F.A.I.T.H. (Forsaking All, I Trust Him), my Anchor was stronger.

I AM a living, breathing, walking, talking, moving miracle woman of God. The storm of cancer may have been a passing cyclone in my life, not to disrupt it, but to clear the path for my faith to make me whole!

As for me, cancer was put on notice and was forever canceled!

Lord thank you for teaching me how to choose the road of Faith.

BRIDGET
SHAW

Bridget Shaw is married to Kenneth Shaw, and they have two adult children, Kayla Shaw, and Joshua Shaw.

Bridget is the founder of The Dream BIG K & B Area LLC. Under the Dream BIG umbrella, Bridget and her husband, Ken, enjoy supplying affordable housing for their community. In addition, Bridget enjoys sharing God's word through speaking engagements. She reminds women all things are possible through Christ and that women are needed in the business world. Bridget also continues building in Direct Sales and coaching others in their business goals. In her role as an Independent National Sales Director, Bridget coaches thousands of women across the country, taking them from the beginning stages of business to Next Level. Bridget has been featured in several magazines: The National Applause Magazine and The Start Something Beautiful Magazine. She is also an international trainer working in many markets.

Bridget sits on the board of The C.A.N Foundation INC. As a first lady, Bridget creates opportunities for open dialog, allowing others to build a relationship with Christ and fellow Christians. When asked what is her superpower, she says her strong Faith in God - standing on Proverbs 3:5-6.

Contact Information:
BridgetLshaw@comcast.net
(843) 697-4993
IG: bridgetshaw_nsd
FB: bridget.shaw.923

FAITH MAKES ALL THINGS POSSIBLE

by Bridget Shaw

God's Promise to me was all I needed. Yes, my faith was tested but I knew I could trust God.

Raising a man-child proved to be more challenging than my daughter. Not so much because he was a man but because he was strong-willed and determined to chart his own path. Where my home was quiet and in order, he created chaos and concern. This proved to be also in God's plan because it made me rely that much more on my faith.

I am speaking fondly of my son, Joshua Shaw. The challenge started when he was in fourth grade. Calls from school of his unruly behavior, calls from school because he refused to sit down on the bus. Honestly, he challenged everyone. This carried over to hanging out with kids that had lifestyles different from my family. Joshua would sneak out in the middle of the night riding his bike through the neighborhood. A brown boy in Hanahan after midnight was not favorable.

My husband and I were at a loss. With our daughter Kayla, it was a cakewalk. She didn't test the rules and was very good at keeping the tempo that was established. Joshua would remind us often and with pride that he was not Kayla. It was a constant struggle, but I continued to believe God.

My husband Ken and I would pray to God for Joshua. We started kneeling by Joshua's bed when he wasn't home praying for God to intervene. Joshua was required to attend church with us and not church with the neighborhood kids. We kept him close. We insisted that he participate in the church service. He would read scripture and usher. We prayed at the breakfast table. We prayed at the dinner table. We prayed before bed. The praying was with Josh and for Josh and over Josh. I didn't know how to change Joshua, but I knew God did. I knew if he would turn and build a relationship with the Father, he would change. I wasn't looking to make him like Kayla. God had given him a certain set of skills that would later define him. I didn't want the enemy to use those skills and that required Joshua to know God.

This faith walk continued for 5 years. Finally, there was a break. I found Josh not to be where he said he was, and I left the house to find him. He got back a few seconds before me and I caught him in the stairway.

I was so angry, and I began to fight with my words and my hands. He didn't respond; he went to his room.

The next morning when Joshua came downstairs, he was a different person. It seemed sudden. We noticed him not asking to hang out with questionable friends. He wasn't alone in his room as much and wanted to interact with the family. Even school changed for him. He was participating in class and the calls from his teachers went from bad news to great reports.

I asked him what happened. What brought about this character adjustment? He said that he talked to God because he didn't want to be the person he had become anymore.

Josh's change appeared to be instant, but the consequences of this unfavorable behavior would begin to unfold. Not everyone was willing to accept the change in my son. He was still labeled as undesirable because of his past behavior. We refused the labels and we insisted that he be allowed to prove himself. We had to show our faith because we wanted Josh to see how to rely fully on God - no matter what it looked like.

While Joshua was building his relationship with Christ, we tried many things. We wanted him to experience God in all parts of life. He took music lessons to soothe himself. He joined Christian Athletes to help with his communication skills and sports. We wanted him to change his circle and be around young people who knew God. All these things helped in different ways. He was good at baseball, track, and wrestling but his sport was football. This gave him focus and still taught him that his faith in God was crucial and important in every area of his life.

He had not put much into school and his grades reflected his lack of focus. Now, he is in the 11th grade. Our country shuts down because of Covid. This is when colleges should have been calling him. Joshua now must deal with the consequences of the past. He is excelling in football, but his GPA is at rock bottom.

All the years of covering this kid in prayer and keeping him in the presence of God, allowed him to now call on God himself and his faith made him UNSTOPPABLE. Joshua Shaw was able to transfer the same discipline he had on the field to the classroom. He took his 1.8 GPA and turned it into a 3.6 GPA. Even with the improvement in school, Joshua had ZERO offers for college football. This was heartbreaking to watch.

We told him to trust God. We told him to remember God wants us to rely on Him for everything and that every part of our lives is important to Him. As his faith grew and he was able to totally rely on God, we watched God reveal 8 offers. As the offers started to come in, I told Josh to ask God what was right for him. I wanted Josh to have God's total approval. Joshua Shaw ended up with a Full Football Scholarship to South Carolina State University.

God is so faithful. He aligned the right people and the perfect timing to fulfill Joshua's dream of playing D1 football. Proverbs 16:3 tells us... Commit unto the Lord all that you do, and your plans will succeed. Looking at the beginning, Joshua would appear to be like so many others. Great talent but unable to meet the requirements to get into college. I know that it was our faith as a family that opened the doors for this amazing opportunity. We only allowed ourselves to see what God would do. We believed that God would have the final word. Given the chance, we agreed to give God all the credit for His grace and mercy.

I always knew in Faith all things are possible. As a mother, I could not trust the naked eye. I covered my son in prayer and even though it was impossible for victory through the lens of men, I knew God had promised to do more than I could imagine.

I challenge you to look at what God has already done in your life. I dare you to visit those chapters in your life when you felt alone. God was there. Those early years when you didn't know God, but others had prayed for you, and you walked on the stacked-up prayers of parents and grandparents. He was there. It is that kind of radical faith that allows you to see things that seemed impossible unfold in your life.

In the end, changing Josh wasn't the answer. He was exactly who God made him to be. The answer was Josh knowing God for himself and Josh allowing God to use him and not allowing the enemy to peep into his life. He was supposed to create chaos. He was supposed to chart his own way. He is a Change Agent.

I am so glad that I knew that faith would make all things possible!

NORA'S FAVORITE QUOTES

Faith is defined as complete trust or confidence in someone or something. May these quotes inspire you to have faith on your journey of greatness.

"Through hard work, perseverance and a faith in God, you can live your dreams."
- Ben Carson

To have faith is to trust yourself to the water. When you swim you don't grab hold of the water, because if you do you will sink and drown. Instead, you relax, and float."
- Alan Watts

"When you have faith in God, you don't have to worry about the future. You just know it's all in His hands. You just go to and do your best."
- Elder Bryan Mathison

"Believe in yourself, and the rest will fall into place. Have faith in your own abilities, work hard, and there is nothing you cannot accomplish."
- Brad Henry

"Faith is unseen but felt, faith is strength when we feel we have none, faith is hope when all seems lost."
- Catherine Pulsifer

"Walk in confidence, be proud, and most importantly have faith in God."
- Dr. Nora Shariff- Borden

"Whatever you want in life, other people are going to want it too. Believe in yourself enough to accept the idea that you have an equal right to it."
- Diane Sawyer

"The smallest seed of faith is better than the largest fruit of happiness."
- Henry David Thoreau

NORA'S FAVORITE QUOTES

"No matter what has happened to you in the past or what is going on in your life right now, it has no power to keep you from having an amazingly good future if you will walk by faith in God. God loves you! He wants you to live with victory over sin so you can possess His promises for your life today!"
- Joyce Meyer

"A grateful heart is a beginning of greatness. It is an expression of humility. It is a foundation for the development of such virtues as prayer, faith, courage, contentment, happiness, love, and well-being."
- James E. Faust

"Faith that it's not always in your hands or things don't always go the way you planned, but you have to have faith that there is a plan for you, and you must follow your heart and believe in yourself no matter what."
- Martina McBride

"I believe if you keep your faith, you keep your trust, you keep the right attitude, if you're grateful, you'll see God open up new doors."
- Joel Osteen

"And whatever you ask in prayer, you will receive, if you have faith."
- Matthew 21:22, The Bible

"Faith and prayer are the vitamins of the soul; man cannot live in health without them."
- Mahalia Jackson

"My faith didn't remove the pain, but it got me through the pain. Trusting God didn't diminish or vanquish the anguish, but it enabled me to endure it."
- Robert Roger

"Believe in yourself when nobody else does."
- Mary J. Blige

"Every day you need to get a full dose of the Word and meditate on scripture, and if you discipline yourself and remain consistent, your faith will grow and mature, and remember that God, the Word, and your faith, are a recipe for success."
- Stephanie Williams

NORA'S FAVORITE QUOTES

"Hearing how God is moving in other places encourages and inspires our faith for what God wants to do in our own corner of the world."
- Matt Brown

"If you have a good support system like your family and your friends around you, then you can't go wrong. So just believe in yourself, do you your thing, and stay strong in what you believe in."
- Roman Reigns

"You can have whatever you want if you believe in yourself and keep your feet firmly planted in the ground."
- A.J. McLean

"Technology is nothing. What's important is that you have a faith in people, that they're basically good and smart, and if you give them tools, they'll do wonderful things with them."
- Steve Jobs

"Always believe in yourself and keep going. You don't have to have the most talent in the world. You don't have to be the smartest person in the world. If you persist and you persist and you persist, you will be successful."
- Dean Cain

"If you believe in yourself and feel confident in yourself, you can do anything. I really believe that."
- Karlie Kloss

"I believe that God has put gifts and talents and ability on the inside of every one of us. When you develop that and you believe in yourself and you believe that you're a person of influence and a person of purpose, I believe you can rise up out of any situation."
- Joel Osteen

"It's important to believe in yourself and the beauty of your dreams and to not let anyone tell you different."
- Victoria Arlen

NORA'S FAVORITE QUOTES

"Believe in yourself! Have faith in your abilities! Without a humble but reasonable confidence in your own powers you cannot be successful or happy."
- Norman Vincent Peale

"Faith is a living, daring confidence in God's grace, so sure and certain that a man could stake his life on it a thousand times."
- Martin Luther

"The greatest legacy one can pass on to one's children and grandchildren is not money or other material things accumulated in one's life, but rather a legacy of character and faith."
- Billy Graham

"Keep faith. The most amazing things in life tend to happen right at the moment you're about to give up hope."
- Anonymous

"Faith. It's all about believing. You don't know how it will happen. But you know it will."
- Anonymous

"Your faith can move mountains and your doubt can create them."
- Anonymous

"Your hardest times often lead to the greatest moments of your life. Keep the faith. It will all be worth it in the end."
- Anonymous

"Faith does not make things easy; it makes them possible."
- Anonymous

"Sometimes the best thing you can do is not think, not wonder, not imagine, not obsess. Just breath and have faith that everything will work out for the best."
- Anonymous

"Faith is like WIFI. It's invisible, but it has the power to connect you to what you need."
- Anonymous

NORA'S FAVORITE QUOTES

"True peace comes from knowing that God is in control."
    - Anonymous

"Let your faith be bigger than your fear."
    - Anonymous

"Surrender to what is. Let go of what was. Have faith in what will be."
    - Sonia Ricotti

"Only in the darkness can you see the stars."
    - Martin Luther King Jr.

"Don't worry. God is always on time. Trust him."
    - Anonymous

"If one has faith, one has everything."
    - Ramakrishna

"We walk by faith, not by sight."
    - Anonymous

"Faith is seeing light with your heart when all your eyes see is darkness."
    - Anonymous

"Always pray to have eyes that see the best in people, a heart that forgives the worst, a mind that forgets the bad, and a soul that never loses faith in God."
    - Anonymous

"Feed your faith and your fear will starve."
    - Anonymous

"The principal part of faith is patience."
    - George MacDonald

"When you have come to the edge, faith is knowing you will be taught to fly."
    - Anonymous

NORA'S FAVORITE QUOTES

"Faith is taking the first step even when you don't see the whole staircase."
   - Martin Luther King Jr.

"Faith is unseen but felt, faith is strength when we feel we have none, faith is hope when all seems lost."
   - Catherine Pulsifer

"Fear looks, Faith Jumps"
   - Smith Wigglesworth

"It's time to have bold faith."
   - Anonymous

"Faith is a choice to trust God even when the road ahead seems uncertain."
   - Dave Willis

"When you have faith in yourself you don't need others to believe in you."
   - Anonymous

"Faith moves mountains, but you have to keep pushing while you are praying."
   - Henry David Thoreau

"If you lose faith, you lose all."
   - Eleanor Roosevelt

"Faith is a recognition of those things which are above the sense."
   - Henry Ward Beech

"Faith is a passionate intuition."
   - William Wordsworth

"Faith it until you make it."
   - Anonymous

"Doubt your doubts before you doubt your faith."
   - Dieter F. Uchtdorf

NORA'S FAVORITE QUOTES

"There isn't enough room in your mind for both worry and faith. You must decide which one will live there."
> - Anonymous

"Choose faith instead of fear and life will become a lot more fun."
> - Dave Willis

"Faith comes from within."
> - ATGW

"Your future is as bright as your faith."
> - Anonymous

"When you have faith, it makes all things possible."
> - Dr. Nora Shariff -Borden

"Faith is the key that unlocks the door to your greatness."
> - Dr. Nora Shariff-Borden

"Great things happen when people have Great Faith accompanied with great expectations!"
> - Dr. Nora Shariff-Borden

"Depending on God for your faith and wellbeing will help you out of the darkest places!"
> - Dr. Nora Shariff- Borden

"If fear is cultivated it will become stronger, if faith is cultivated it will achieve mastery."
> - John Paul Jones

"Faith is the bird that feels the light when the dawn is still dark."
> - Rabindranath Tagore

"To one who has faith, no explanation is necessary. To one without faith, no explanation is possible."
> - Thomas Aquinas

NORA'S FAVORITE QUOTES

"Be faithful in small things because it is in them that your strength lies."
- Mother Teresa

"When you focus on being a blessing, God makes sure that you are always blessed in abundance."
- Joel Osteen

"I am far from being what I want to be, but I have faith in God who will help me to succeed."
- Dr. Nora Shariff-Borden

"We are never defeated unless we give up on God."
- Ronald Reagan

"We are twice armed if we fight with faith."
- Plato

"Faith consists in believing when it is beyond the power of reason to believe."
- Voltaire

"Faith is not belief without proof, but trust without reservation."
- D. Elton Trueblood

"Faith is an oasis in the heart which will never be reached by the caravan of thinking."
- Khalil Gibran

"A casual stroll through the lunatic asylum shows that faith does not prove anything."
- Friedrich Nietzsche

"God will never give you anything you can't handle, so don't stress."
- Kelly Clarkson

"Love, hope, fear, faith - these make humanity; These are its sign and note and character."
- Robert Browning

NORA'S FAVORITE QUOTES

"Every tomorrow has two handles. We can take hold of it with the handle of anxiety or the handle of faith. "
>   - Henry Ward Beecher

"Resist your fear; fear will never lead you to a positive end. Go for your faith and what you believe."
>   - Bishop T. D. Jakes

"God enters by a private door into every individual."
>   - Ralph Waldo Emerson

"There are many things that are essential to arriving at true peace of mind, and one of the most important is faith, which cannot be acquired without prayer."
>   - John Wooden

"I have come to the conclusion that the most important element in human life is faith."
>   - Rose Kennedy

"We can no more do without spirituality than we can do without food, shelter, or clothing."
>   - Ernest Holmes

"In my deepest, darkest moments, what really got me through was a prayer. Sometimes my prayer was 'Help me.' Sometimes a prayer was 'Thank you.' What I've discovered is that intimate connection and communication with my creator will always get me through because I know my support, my help, is just a prayer away."
>   - Iyanla Vanzant

"It takes vision and courage to create - it takes faith and courage to prove."
>   - Owen D. Young

"When you have faith in God, you become confident that everything is clear."
>   - Dr. Nora Shariff-Borden

NORA'S FAVORITE QUOTES

"Of all duties, prayer certainly is the sweetest and most easy."
- Laurence Sterne

"Faith gives you an inner strength and a sense of balance and perspective in life."
- Gregory Peck

"He wants you all to Himself to put His loving, divine arms around you."
- Charles Stanley

"He who has faith has... an inward reservoir of courage, hope, confidence, calmness, and assuring trust that all will come out well - even though to the world it may appear to come out most badly."
- Unknown

"Faith in oneself is the best and safest course."
- Michelangelo

"To me faith means not worrying."
- John Dewey

"God didn't make a mistake when He made you. You need to see yourself as God sees you."
- Joel Osteen

"As your faith is strengthened you will find that there is no longer the need to have a sense of control, that things will flow as they will, and that you will flow with them, to your great delight and benefit."
- Emmanuel Teney

"Your faith is the only safe ground you should stand on!"
- Dr. Nora Shariff-Borden

"Believe in yourself, in the power you have to control your own life, day by day, believe in the strength that you have deep inside, and your faith will help show you the way. Believe in tomorrow and what it will bring; let a hopeful heart carry you through, for things will work out if you trust and believe there's no limit to what you can do."
- Emily Matthews

CONTRIBUTING WRITERS' FAVORITE QUOTES

DR. JACQUELINE MOHAIR
"Let your life reflect the faith you have in God. Fear nothing and pray about everything. Be strong, trust God's word, and trust the process."
- Germany Kent

"Faith is the strength by which a shattered world shall emerge into light."
- Helen Keller

DR. RENEE HUFFMAN
"Faith is taking the first step, even when you don't see the whole staircase."
- Martin Luther king. Jr. - iamfearlesssoul.com

"'Crazy Faith' is thoughts and actions that lack reason but trusting fully in what you cannot explicitly prove."
- Mike Todd

CHERYL MORGAN WILSON
"Nothing beats a failure but a try."
- Cheryl Morgan Wilson

"There's nothing new under the sun, everything that is was, and everything that was is."
- Eccles. 1:9

REV. DR. STEPHANIE CASTRO
"It's better to be a lion for a day than a sheep all your life."
- Elizabeth Kenny

"Our deepest fear is not that we are inadequate. Our deepest fear is that we are powerful beyond measure."
- Marianne Williamson

CONTRIBUTING WRITERS' FAVORITE QUOTES

DR. HARRIET ROBERSON
"I've learned that people will forget what you said, people will forget what you did, but people will never forget how you made them feel."
- Maya Angelou

"Success isn't about how much money you make, it's about the difference you make in people's lives."
- Michelle Obama

DR. ANGELA BENNETT
"Character cannot be developed in ease and quiet. Only through experience of trial and suffering can the soul be strengthened, ambition inspired, and success achieved."
- Helen Keller

"If you're always trying to be normal, you will NEVER know how amazing you can be."
- Maya Angelou

DR. BARBARA JACKSON
"My mission in life is not merely to survive, but to thrive; and to do so with some passion, some compassion, some humor, and some style."
- Maya Angelou
"They may forget your name, but they will never forget how you made them feel."
- Maya Angelou

GLYNNIS THATCH
"Ignore the glass ceiling and do your work. If you're focusing on the glass ceiling, focusing on what you don't have, focusing on the limitations, then you will be limited."
- Ava Duvernay

"People will forget what you said, people will forget what you did, but people will never forget how you made them feel."
- Maya Angelou

CONTRIBUTING WRITERS' FAVORITE QUOTES

MEKITA WHTIFIELD
"I can do all things through Christ who strengthens me."
    - Philippians 4:13

"Education is the key to success in life, and teachers make a lasting impression on their students."
    - Solomon Ortiz

DR. UZO OSILI
"To forgive is to set a prisoner free and discover that the prisoner was you."
    - Lewis B. Smedes

"Let us not become weary in doing good for at the proper time we will reap a harvest if we don't give up."
    - Gal 6:9

DR. CYNTHIA MAXIE MILTON
"If you fall, fall on your back because if you can look up, you can get up!"
    - Les Brown

"Life is not just about you, it is about what can be done through you to positively impact the lives of others."
    - Dr. Cynthia Maxie Milton

DR. PAMELA D. HARVEY-COX
"Believing in yourself is not for you; it's for every person who has touched your life in a significant way and for every person your life will touch the same way five minutes from now, or five centuries from now."
    - Joye Miller

"A believer...is never disturbed because other persons do not see the fact which he sees."
    - Ralph Waldo Emerson.

CONTRIBUTING WRITERS' FAVORITE QUOTES

DR. LONDON SPIVEY
"If it comes, let it. If it goes, let it."
- Nicholas Sparks

"We don't see things as they are, we see them as we are."
- Anais Nin

SONJI NEVERSON
"Don't give up because God's Love & Glory is always there and will Never Ever Fail."
- Unknown

"Never Give Up and Never Give in."
- Hal Newhouser

ARDRA SINETT
"Belief is the Beginning"
- Ardra Sinett

"All things work together for the good of those who love God."
- Romans 8:28

DR. LISA YVETTE JONES
"For we are God's handiwork, created in Christ Jesus to do good works, which God prepared in advance for us to do."
- Ephesians 2:10, KJV

"But he was wounded for our transgressions, he was bruised for our iniquities: the chastisement of our peace was upon him, and with his stripes, we are healed."
- Isaiah 53:5, KJV

CONTRIBUTING WRITERS' FAVORITE QUOTES

BRIDGET SHAW
"Now unto him that is able to do exceedingly abundantly above all that we ask or think, according to the power that worketh in us,"
- Ephesians 3:20 KJV

"Trust in the LORD with all thine heart; And lean not unto thine own understanding. In all thy ways acknowledge him, and He shall direct thy paths."
- Proverbs 3:5-6 KJV

DAILY AFFIRMATION:
I HAVE FAITH IN GOD'S LOVE FOR ME

by Pastor Andre' Gorham

I have faith that God loves me. I am not just some tool in His shed. I am the apple of His eye. I am why He died on the cross, was raised from the dead, and sits on the right hand of the Father.

I am super special in His eyes. I am just as important as any mission trip, Tv ministry, church ministry, or giving ministry. Just like I am there for others, He is there for me, and He has others there for me. I am valuable to God also. He loves me like He loves the entire world. He has money for me. He has nothing but good for me. He brings the best people to me. He meets all my needs and desires.

He celebrates me, appreciates me, and compensates me.

He has love, joy, peace, goodness, strength, wisdom, health, favor, and victory for me. He makes things easy for me. He removes obstacles for me. I am His beloved. There is nothing wrong with me. I have "Christ" esteem. I feel good about who I am in Him. I see myself in Him. I am not afraid; He is here now.

I believe God that I am super healthy, and I am a healthy weight. I believe God that my youth is renewed like eagles. I believe in God that I have a sound mind. I believe in God that my soul, emotions, and will is strong. I believe in God that I have great peace. I have eternal life in Christ because of Him.

I am clear that I am not alone. I love me like God loves me. I see me like God sees me. I think about myself as God thinks about me. I feel about me like God feels about me. I do good things for myself, like I do good things for others.

God doesn't take advantage of me. He takes care of me. He has positioned me for greatness. Because of Him, I am above and not beneath. His plan for me is a good plan. He thinks thoughts of peace about me and brings me expected peace. I am clear about His plans for me. Knowing God is a blessing to me.

Surely, goodness and mercy shall follow me all the days of my life. Thank You, God. You have restored my soul. I am refreshed and rejuvenated in

His love. God is 100% for me at all times. Every hour of the day, Jesus is my best friend.

He has opened His good treasure unto me. He has set me on high. He has made me the head and not the tail. He protects me from bad things and bad people. He always keeps me. My enemies are His enemies. My issues are His issues. Because God has me, I am in a very healthy relationship with my God. God truly loves me.

CPSIA information can be obtained
at www.ICGtesting.com
Printed in the USA
JSHW020428271222
35342JS00004B/10

9 780996 924696